James

A Visual and Textual Guide

Also available in the High Definition Commentary Series:

Romans: A Visual and Textual Guide

Philippians: A Visual and Textual Guide

Also available from Steven E. Runge:

Lexham Discourse Hebrew Bible

Lexham High Definition Old Testament

Discourse Studies and Biblical Interpretation:

A Festschrift in Honor of Stephen H. Levinsohn

Introducing New Testament Discourse Grammar: Video Series

Discourse Grammar of the Greek New Testament:
A Practical Introduction for Teaching and Exegesis

Lexham Discourse Greek New Testament

Lexham High Definition New Testament

Visit Logos.com/Runge to learn more

James

A Visual and Textual Guide

High Definition Commentary

Steven E. Runge

LEXHAM PRESS

James: A Visual and Textual Guide
High Definition Commentary

Lexham Press, 1313 Commercial St., Bellingham, WA 98225
LexhamPress.com

ISBN 978-1-57-799630-9

Visual Design: Josh Warren
Lexham Editorial Team: Rebecca Brant, Abigail Stocker
Cover Design: Shiloh Hubbard
Typesetting: ProjectLuz.com

Acknowledgments and Dedication

The James volume of the High Definition Commentary series marked the beginning of a new partnership with a talented graphic artist, Josh Warren of Faithlife. Through his patience and persistence, we were able forge a solid working relationship. To Josh go the kudos for the graphics. I would also like to thank the gifted and supportive team at Lexham Press who have shepherded this volume through the publication process. Rebecca, Justin, Lynnea, and Abigail, thanks so much for your professionalism and attention to detail. Lastly, I want to acknowledge a voice I often hear when reading James, a practical example of faith in action whom I'm humbled to call my friend and brother in Christ: Wayne Key. Wayne exudes the characteristic practicality of the upper Midwest coupled with a deep commitment to healthy churches—both instilled in him by his church-planting father. After an impressive career at Boeing, Wayne began (or more truthfully continued) a second one, mentoring struggling churches back to healthy ministry. I had the privilege of shadowing him during a very pivotal time in my walk with Christ. He wisely and graciously helped me to see something God had for me that I'm not sure I would have found without him: a calling as a practical scholar. I most gratefully dedicate this volume to Wayne; thanks so much for investing in me.

Table of Contents

Introduction

How Is the High Definition Commentary Different?

What you are about to read is derived from a rigorous discourse analysis of the Greek text of James. Discourse analysis doesn't look just at what is said, but how it's said. By looking at how James phrased things in Greek, we can see the progression of his thoughts. The phrasing of every sentence in the New Testament presupposes decisions about communication—the same kinds of decisions we make every day.

In this commentary, I lead you through the linguistic devices James used and show what we can learn from them. It's a guided tour of the Greek text—highlighting important issues without getting into all of the nitty-gritty details.

Why I Wrote This Commentary

Commentaries either give you the big picture or all the detail. But I think what most of us really want is a commentary that gives the details we need without losing sight of the big picture. That's what this commentary strives for.

In the *Lexham Discourse Greek New Testament* and the *Lexham High Definition New Testament*, I annotated the significant discourse devices that aid us in biblical interpretation. These volumes have one drawback: They place the responsibility on *you* to synthesize the data into a cohesive analysis. In this volume, I synthesize the conclusions that can be drawn from my analysis of James and make them easy to understand.

Discourse studies have a reputation for complexity. Some joke that it rivals nuclear fission or brain surgery. But here's a secret: As a speaker of *any* language, you actually know a lot more about discourse devices than you might imagine. We rarely think about these issues—we just do what makes most sense to communicate our message.

The Power of Discourse Analysis

Choice implies meaning. If I choose to say something this way as opposed to that way, I must have a reason for doing so. While my analysis of the Greek New Testament and descriptions of discourse devices in the Discourse Grammar of the Greek New Testament equipped me to write this commentary, I do not claim to know what James was thinking or what he had in mind as he wrote. Instead, I operate on the assumption that our use of language is based on our communication objectives. If we use a particular device that usually accomplishes a certain effect, then we can assume the biblical writers used language in the same way. Context is the final arbiter.

Most commentaries provide the scholar's interpretive conclusions using statements like "James is doing [fill in the blank] here." They give you the conclusion, but they don't show you how they got there. This commentary helps you understand what is going on under the hood, linguistically speaking.

The primary job of pastors and teachers is exposition: drawing out the meaning of the text so that we can all faithfully apply it to our lives. When I teach, my goal is not just to give you the answers; it's to teach you how to find the answers. The same is true of this commentary. I will help you understand the flow of James' argument so you can see how the pieces fit together as a whole. I want you to learn how to find the answers on your own and be able to teach others—whether in a small group, a Bible study, a class, or in a sermon.

Why Graphics?

Graphics represent ideas well, especially complex ideas. The graphics in this commentary explain the text and help you (and others) retain its meaning.

Explaining

While the graphics in this commentary help you better understand a passage, the real audience for them is the person you are teaching. The slides help you explain key ideas using something other than a translation or a verbal description. They do not replace those resources, but they serve as another tool in your tool belt.

Retaining

Good graphics pay dividends into the future. Visual aids help us correlate and recall information. How many times have your long-forgotten memories been triggered by an old photo? We may not completely understand how the mind works, but visual signposts play a role in retention and recall. Most passages in this commentary have several graphics tied to a key idea. Some break down a complex idea into steps; others present a difficult idea in a new, memorable way.

How to Use the Graphics

As a message closes, there is the inevitable "So what?" question. The slides accompanying this commentary will help you answer that question. The slides can help you do more than just make as point as you are teaching. You can also repeat a graphic used earlier in your message in your conclusion and application. It will not only trigger memories, but it will help people retain information. The same holds true when you review graphics from previous weeks. Like flashbacks in TV shows, repeating the graphic associated with a key idea will trigger memories. Just a brief glimpse stimulates greater recall than using a verbal summary.

My Goal for This Commentary

I want you to better understand why James wrote his letter and how he organized it. I hope doing so changes your life like it has mine.

> The electronic edition of the *High Definition Commentary: James* is available for Logos Bible Software and includes ready-to-use versions of all the graphics for use in Proclaim, PowerPoint, and Keynote. You'll find it online at **Logos.com/HDCommentary**.

James 1

James 1:1–11

The greeting of a New Testament epistle plays an important grounding role for the letter that follows, so it's important we pay close attention to how James frames his greeting. It does more than objectively identify the writer (James) and the intended audience (the church; e.g., "From James, to the Church"). Greetings in the New Testament letters generally offer a thematically loaded portrait of each party. The first part characterizes the writer (e.g., "Paul, an apostle of Christ Jesus" in Colossians 1:1). The second part characterizes the recipients of the letter, the intended audience (e.g., "the saints and faithful brothers in Christ in Colossae," Col 1:2). The nature of these portraits varies from letter to letter, and seems to be based on the nature of the message that follows.

Think about how we use introductions today. Just imagine that I was being introduced as a speaker at a Bible conference somewhere. What would people think if the emcee introduced me as "Ruth and Abby's dad" or "the associate editor of the Fourth Corner Fly Fishing Club newsletter" without any reference to my academic credentials? Although I am a dad and associate editor of a newsletter, these credentials have no relevance to the task at hand, Bible teaching. The audience would want some assurance that I was a credible teacher, like hearing about my doctoral degree, my position as scholar-in-residence, or the books I have authored. It is not a matter of choosing *any* credential, but choosing the one that best suits the specific context.

Switching back to greetings in New Testament letters, the people receiving the letters already knew the author, at least by reputation if not by personal interaction. The letters were also carried by hand rather than sent through some delivery service like today, and the letter-bearer could clarify the identity of the sender. So we need to look at the greetings as serving a greater purpose than identifying sender and receiver. James intentionally paints thematic portraits that shape how his readers would have viewed him and, even, themselves. From our modern standpoint, the portraits chosen narrow the possible ways we might view James or those to whom he is writing.

Think about some of the possible credentials that the writer James could have chosen for his greeting in verse 1. Most scholars believe he was Jesus' own brother; reminding his readers of this fact would certainly have boosted his credibility in their eyes. James was also an apostle and prominent enough in the Jerusalem church to chair the first church council (Acts 15:6–21). He was also one of the leaders to whom Paul presented his gospel for an orthodoxy check (Acts 9:26–29; Gal 1:18–2:10). James potentially could have cited any of these credentials to establish his authority for the claims and exhortations he makes in his letter.

James Who?: As the brother of Jesus and apostle of the church in Jerusalem, James had more prestigious credentials to draw upon than "servant of God." James' choice to select humility over a high honor sets the tone for his treatment of power and position in the rest of the letter.

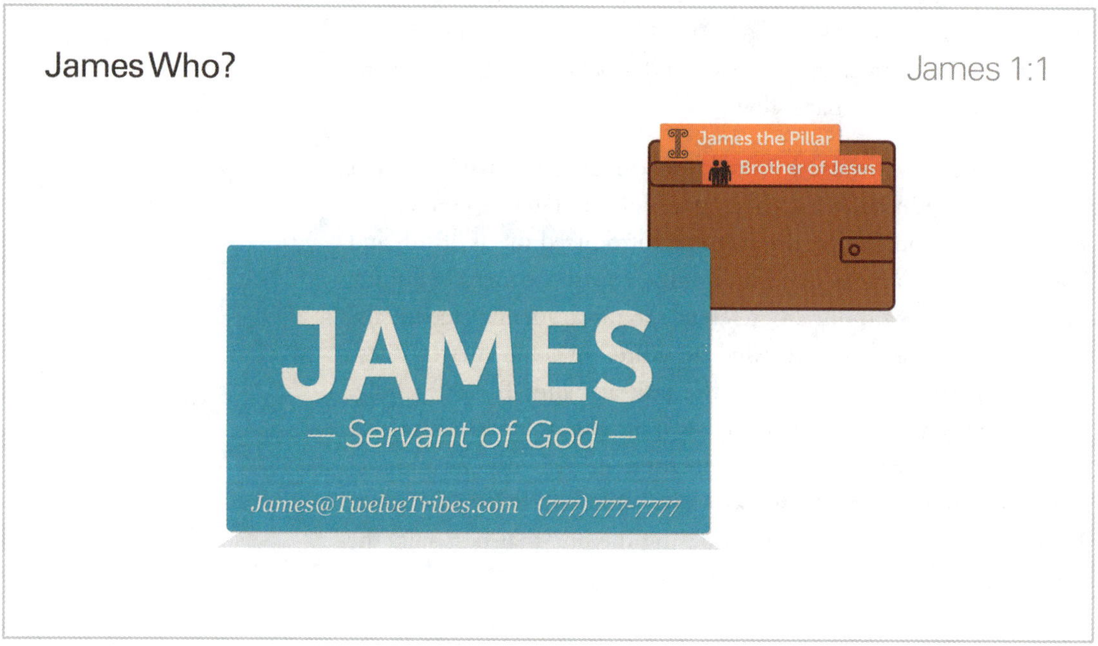

So which credential does James choose? How does he want his readers to think about him? Not what we might think: James introduces himself as a servant rather than an esteemed leader. James—the servant of God and of the Lord Jesus Christ—gives us a hint about the thematic role that status and position will play in this letter.

James does more than call himself a servant; he calls attention to something else here in the introduction. In the Greek, James changes the word order to emphasize the two masters he serves. The phrase "of God and of the Lord Jesus Christ" is placed before "servant" in Greek to emphasize it—not something we can see in English. This use of emphasis typically signals that a wrong idea is being corrected; i.e., he is the servant of God and the Lord Jesus Christ, not someone else. This further reinforces James' humble introduction of himself.

The second part of the greeting—identifying the audience—paints a thematic portrait, just like the first part. Rather than addressing them as "the church in ____" (1 Cor 1:2; 2 Cor 1:1; Gal 1:2) or as "the saints in ___" (see Rom 1:7; Eph 1:1; Phil 1:1), he refers to them as the "twelve tribes." Ostensibly this means the tribes of the nation of Israel, hearkening back to the Old Testament characterization of God's people. James also tacks on an additional description, packaged separately in Greek from the twelve tribes. This description characterizes his readers as the ones scattered or dispersed. In other words, James is not addressing a specific group in a particular city, but believers from the "twelve tribes" who have been scattered because of Roman persecution. The lack of a specific audience in the greeting has led scholars to call James, Hebrews, and the letters of Peter and John the "General Letters." Even though we don't know where these readers are, the "twelve tribes" terminology is decidedly Jewish compared to the more generic "church" or "saints" used in Paul's letters. James' designation for his audience fits with the themes contained in his letter, as well as his references to the Old Testament.

Verse 2 marks the transition from the greeting to the main part of the letter, called the body. James begins with an exhortation to consider *something* all joy, but he frames his statement so as to delay disclosing exactly what this something is. How? He has already identified the audience as the twelve scattered tribes, yet he reidentifies them as "dear brothers." Think about it: Is he really only talking to the "dear brothers" of the scattered tribes? No. Since this new expression doesn't narrow down the audience or switch to a new one, James could have left it out.

So why include this extra reference? There are two reasons. First, even though this expression doesn't provide much new detail about the audience, it still recharacterizes them as family, beloved members instead of the more emotionally detached "scattered tribes." Since this expression doesn't switch to a different audience, it acts to recharacterize them.

This leads to the second reason for adding "dear brothers." James' extra reference to his audience interrupts the flow of the sentence, serving as a rhetorical speed bump before something really important. Normally such references to the audience come at the beginning of the sentence, grabbing the attention of some new subset of the broader audience. For instance, in Ephesians 5:22, 25; 6:1, 4, 5, and 9, Paul uses direct address to get the attention of wives, husbands, children, slaves, and masters, respectively. This "shout out" tells the broader audience that what follows is specifically addressed to a subgroup, not necessarily the whole group. That is not the case in

Generic Forms of Direct Address and Gender-Inclusive Language

There has been an ongoing, divisive debate about the merits of using gender-inclusive language in Bible translations. The debate stems from the use of expressions like "my brothers" in James 1:2 to address both male and female members of the audience. There is little doubt that these expressions were considered gender-neutral to the original audience. But the open question is how such expressions will be understood today. Are they still gender-neutral, or do they convey chauvinistic overtones? Some argue this common expression should be translated as "my brothers and sisters" so as to explicitly include both genders, as we see in the NIV 2011. Others argue that any such change we might make represents a disregard for the authority of the text. Both of these are valid points, but is there some way forward that respects both? The answer to this question will influence how we read and teach a book like James based on the number of times expressions like this crop up. Although this matter has some complexities, there is indeed a way forward.

We can divide the uses of direct address like "my brothers" into two types: those that are needed to know "who did what to whom," and those that are not needed. For instance, in Ephesians 5:22, 25; 6:1, 4, 5, and 9, Paul directly addresses subgroups of the audience; the direct address signals the switch from the church to wives, then to husbands, to children, to slaves, and then to masters. Without the direct address, we would have a difficult time recognizing Paul's switch to some new subgroup of addressees. These are examples of required uses of direct address; they are "mission-critical" to the text and cannot be changed. Admittedly there are a few instances where one could make a case for or against the need for direct address, but the important thing to recognize is that there are linguistic criteria to guide such usage.

Believe it or not, these necessary uses of direct address represent only a minority of all uses. The majority of direct addresses found in the New Testament are not semantically required. So then what are these other uses of direct address accomplishing? A good many help us identify boundaries in the discourse. When the New Testament was originally written, there were no conventions like punctuation, paragraph breaks, or chapter divisions to help readers know where to divide the text. Redundant forms of direct address are one means writers could use to signal such boundaries. How? Think about how the semantically required addresses operate. Forms of direct address like "wives," "husbands," and "children" signaled the beginning of a new section addressing the new group of people. Using a generic form of address—one that doesn't do anything to change the audience—is a natural extension of the same linguistic device. In colloquial English we use expressions like "bro," "dude," and "man" to do the same thing.

Another use of redundant address operates at a more local level. Instead of signaling a new paragraph, sometimes the expression is found in the middle of a sentence, as in James 1:2. This unneeded direct address creates a speed bump, delaying our reading of what lies on the other side. This delay results in anticipation or suspense, drawing extra attention to what is typically an important thematic statement. So instead of drawing attention to a new addressee or a new section of the discourse, this use in the middle of a clause draws attention to something surprising or important.

If we consider the generic forms of direct address used in languages, most share an interesting trait: They are nearly always masculine. Why? Well, the masculine form of something is most often the generic one; it doesn't limit the gender. I can talk about a female lion or female sheep but not about a male lioness or a male ewe. This isn't linguistic chauvinism; it is simply an economy of language. It is easier to have one form serve double duty (masculine and generic) than to have a third, androgynous form for generic references.

If we look at how Greek hearers would have responded to "brothers," or how modern English-speakers respond to "bro" or "dude," it is doubtful that gender figures significantly into the processing of the term. Although in some communities women address each other as "sister," more often I've heard women calling other women "dude" instead of "dudette" or "dudes." Again, this has nothing to do with linguistic chauvinism and everything to do with the constraints and economy of language.

So how do we move forward in properly handling these generic forms of direct address in James? The call for changing to inclusive forms of address misunderstands the important distinction between required and redundant direct address. If you are going to change terminology—which is a completely legitimate choice—then be sure to choose something that does not create the impression that you are narrowing the audience down to an actual subgroup of people. Plural expressions like "folks," "church," or "family" can play that role but may sound awkward at first. My preferred option when preaching is "folks" because most people are used to hearing it, but it omits the family overtone of "brothers." Whatever you decide to do, keep in mind the reason these redundant forms were used, and do your best not to undermine their important function.

James 1:2 since the expression is too generic to narrow down the audience. The phrase is unnecessary and interrupts the sentence flow—confirmation that "dear brothers" serves a rhetorical function.

Instead of narrowing the scope of the message, the expression in the middle of the sentence creates a speed bump, delaying the disclosure of what James wants us to consider all joy. We use the same kind of delay tactic in English by placing words like "however" in the middle of a thought, usually right before something important or surprising. "The important thing to keep in mind, however, is to ..." What is that important thing? You have to keep reading or listening to find out. Even such a minuscule delay contributes to the suspense of finding out what the speaker is talking about. God has wired us to process language this way, which is why writers like James use devices like this to draw extra attention to important information.

The delay caused by the unneeded direct address gives us a split second to think about the kinds of things we might get overjoyed about. Things like answered prayers might come to mind. An encouraging word from someone or an opportunity to serve others might be worth rejoicing over. But wait, trials? Really? Why in the world would I want to rejoice over those?

Well, it turns out it isn't just the positive mountaintop experiences that grow our faith; verses 3–4 tell us that trials also play an important role. James uses emphasis in the Greek to drive home some important points. We are to consider it *all joy* when these things come along. In other words, we are not supposed to just bow our head down and accept or to just shake our fist at heaven to complain when trials come. Furthermore, this exhortation applies to all kinds of trials we might encounter, not just a select group of them. And instead of having a negative view of trials—as though they were some kind of punishment—James urges us in an unexpected direction, considering them pure joy based on the important role they play in our growth.

In verses 3–4 James elaborates on what's at stake as we choose to rejoice in the midst of trials and describes the resulting effects. He uses "knowing" at the beginning of verse 3 to cast what follows as though it is something we should already understand. Overcoming challenges and enduring trials may not be a lot of fun, but the potential for growth offers a silver lining. The results these trials can bring offer us great incentive for considering them joy. In these verses, James describes a multistep process that begins with trials; in verse 3, he recasts them as a "testing of your faith," which gives us more insight into precisely what he had in mind in verse 2 regarding considering trials all joy.

Consider it What? James 1:2

Consider TRIALS pure joy whenever you encounter them.

Having our faith tested creates endurance. To develop endurance, we must stand under hardship rather than buckling and giving up or trying to avoid the testing. We must sustain this endurance or we will not reach maturity and completeness. In Greek (and translations like the NKJV) the word commonly translated "perfect" occurs twice in verse 4. The first describes the work accomplished by endurance; the second describes one of the outcomes—that we would be perfect/mature. "Perfect" captures the idea of wholeness and completeness rather than moral perfection. James portrays perfection as being all that we were intended to be instead of being a "few bricks shy of a load." God uses trials and testing of our faith as a means of building and growing us to completeness and maturity. James directs us to the bigger picture and the important role they play as faith-builders.

Consider it What?: We might consider many things to be pure joy. James has structured this statement in a way that gives us time to think about these alternatives before learning what he actually has in mind. James' command to consider *trials* pure joy challenges us to rethink what we normally view as a negative thing.

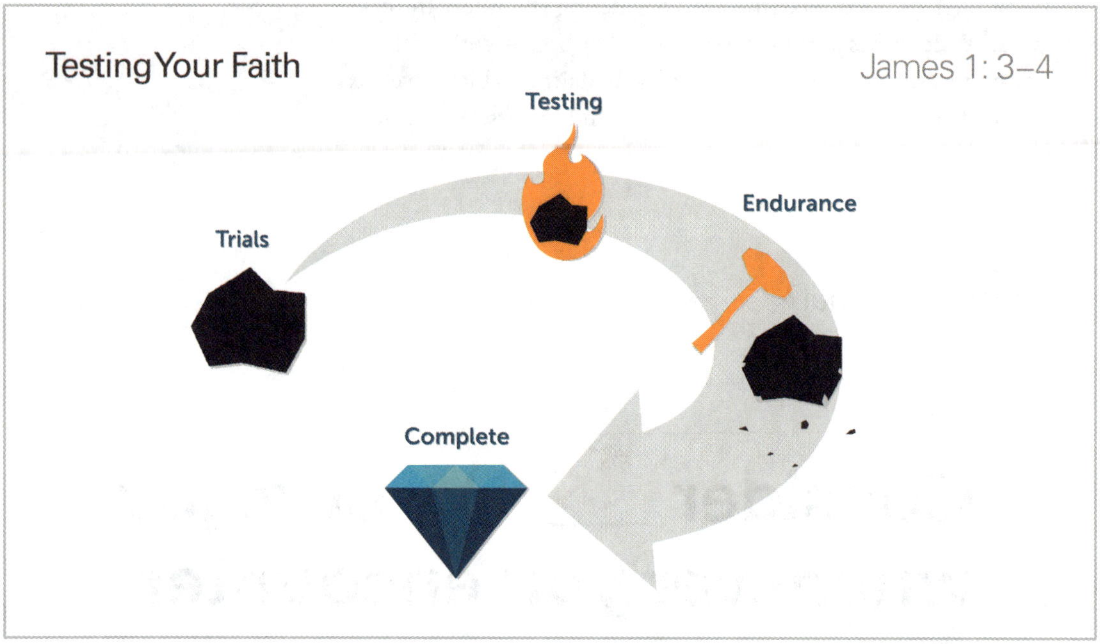

Testing Your Faith:
James describes trials as a process rather than as events. He recharacterizes trials as testing our faith, which in turn builds endurance. Endurance then leads to being perfect—a state James defines as being mature and complete, not lacking anything. Our incentive for persevering in the face of trials is the growth and maturity God brings about through them.

The correlation James makes between testing of faith and spiritual growth is consistent with the principle of testing we find at work elsewhere. Our muscles will atrophy without exercise. Working out by lifting weights tests the muscles, actually tearing them. As they heal, the muscles become stronger and are able to endure more strenuous workouts. Similarly we strengthen our moral character as we face temptation and choose not to give in to our desires. The less we indulge our desires to sin, the more capable of avoiding temptation we become.

James transitions to a new topic in verse 5, asking if there is anyone who lacks wisdom. In spite of this shift in topic, verses 2–4 nevertheless share a close relationship to verse 5. How? Well, verse 4 closes with the notion of completeness and perfection in the sense of "the way it was meant to be." James' transition to lacking wisdom, then, is a test case of sorts, a practical example of the kind of thing someone might be lacking.

Got Wisdom?

James 1:5

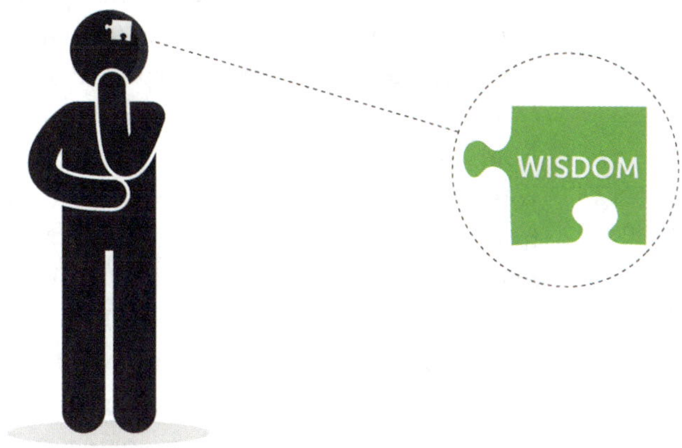

In verse 5 James lets us know that enduring trials will build our faith, but we will have other spiritual needs, like wisdom. The great news is that God will meet those needs as well. Instead of referring to him using a standard expression like "God" or "the Lord," James recharacterizes him as "the One who gives to all without reservation and without reproaching." This shift in names illustrates God's character: He is not going to be upset with us for lacking something, so we don't need to be afraid to ask him for things we need. James portrays God's generosity—he is willing to meet our needs and provide us with what we are missing.

Got Wisdom?: James asks a rhetorical question aimed indirectly at his audience. Instead of asking, "Are you lacking wisdom?," he asks if there is anyone among them who is lacking wisdom. This less-direct approach frames the question more as a hypothetical possibility than as a charge. The goal is to introduce the solution to the problem, not accuse anyone of being unwise.

What James describes in verse 5 sounds great. All we need to do is recognize our need and ask the unreproaching Giver, and he provides it for us, right? Actually, there *is* a catch. Things are not as cut and dried as James makes them sound initially. When James repeats the command to ask in verse 6, he is circling back for a closer look at the matter.

Despite James' encouragement in verse 5 not to be afraid to ask, he offers a more sober presentation of what is involved in verse 6. It is not just a matter of asking for wisdom—we must ask in faith.

He elaborates on the command by offering a negative corollary. Asking in faith means asking without doubting. James underscores this using emphasis in Greek: *in nothing* doubting.

How do asking and doubting relate? James provides a practical illustration on the perils of doubting in the latter half of verse 6, where he likens the doubter to a wave that is blown and tossed about. His conclusion? Doubters should not expect to receive anything from the Lord (verse 7). Think about it: Asking for something you doubt you will receive represents a huge contradiction. James further explores the notion of doubting by describing such a person as double-minded and unstable in all their ways. This reminds me of the character Mr. Facing-Both-Ways from *The Pilgrim's Progress*. He could see the merits of every opinion or option, but he failed to make a decision about which one was superior. If our faith is determined by the arguments for or against something, we too will be swayed as circumstances change. Our faith and confidence must not be built on our own understanding, but on God's proven character (Prov 3:5–6).

Faith vs. Doubt: Although James describes God as generous, giving to us without reservation or reproach, God still demands that we ask in faith, without doubting. James tells us that the person who asks and yet doubts is like the wind-blown surf, a double-minded person who is unstable in all they do. He warns us that if we ask in doubt, we should not expect to receive anything from the Lord.

Fear vs. Doubt

James 1: 6–8

As we will see throughout the book of James, the life of faith is not for the faint of heart. Faith requires us to stand by our decision to trust and obey, despite whatever storms might buffet us. James makes this point clear using the negative example of the double-minded person.

In verses 9–11, James shifts his imagery to contrasting pictures of the lowly and the rich. It almost seems as if he is switching to a new topic, but his affirmation in verse 12 of the person who endures testing suggests that these comments about boasting relate back to the topic of asking in faith. With the exhortations in verses 9–10, James overturns conventional wisdom regarding potential sources for boasting, confidence, and doubt.

James' exhortation for the lowly to boast in their high position takes us off guard because of how it clashes with what we might expect. After all, do you know anyone who revels in lacking high status? Today we use terms like "disenfranchised" or "marginalized" to describe such people, as if they are cut off or set apart from the majority. Contrast these with the metaphors typically associated with those who have authority or money, like being a "powerbroker," a "mover and shaker," or "at the top of the food chain." As we will see in 2:1–4, our tendency is to defer to those with money or position. They are the ones who typically influence society, right? By contrast, the poor and the lowly are rarely shown the same respect as the rich. Instead, they are often treated as invisible, unworthy of our attention. This is the very kind of treatment that James seeks to correct.

How can having a low position be a good thing? James answers by illustrating the fleeting nature of riches. Any confidence we have in wealth instead of in God is not only misplaced, but doomed. James does not say that wealth is bad; he doesn't offer any comment in that regard. His point is that just as wealth is fleeting, so too is the stability it offers. Nevertheless, this shift from valuing wealth and position over people most definitely undermines the prestige our society assigns to them. Conversely, it condemns our treatment of the poor as mistreatment. If we accept his teaching on these matters, it must be reflected in our values and our actions, particularly our (mis)treatment of others based on status.

James pairs his comments about the rich with statements about those in humble positions, suggesting a correlation between lack of status and lack of wealth (see Eccl 9:13–16). Thus, the call for the poor to boast in their high position serves as a backdrop against which Paul contrasts comments about the rich.

So why are the rich to boast in their humiliation? James writes as though it is only a matter of time until their seemingly perfect world falls apart. Hoarding or leveraging riches to gain position and influence over others provides no guarantee for the future. Just as the harsh sun can wither and scorch the grass so that its flowers fail, the power and trappings of riches are short-lived and offer no long-term benefit. Paul leaves the implicit contrast with the poor and the humble unstated. Ostensibly the lack of position or wealth leaves the poor with little else to cling to but their faith in God. In practical terms, there are no competitors for their affection.

Boasting in What Lasts: James compares the short-lived benefit of riches to the flower of grasses. In the same way that the beauty of the flower fails, so too do the luxury and confidence derived from riches. Instead of placing confidence in riches or position, James directs us to place our confidence in that which lasts.

So is James implying that the poor automatically have strong faith, whereas rich folks lack faith? Is he condemning riches as evil or something to be shunned? No. Instead he condemns our apparently timeless human tendency to esteem the rich and treat them with deference (see Jas 2:5–6; 5:1–6). We ought to respect and esteem godly character in others, yet all too often we allow wealth and position to impress us. James here appeals to prototypes—almost caricatures of rich and poor. His goal is for us to reexamine our own sources of confidence and boasting in light of our human tendency to worship wealth instead of the Giver of all good gifts (1:17).

As much as we might say that money doesn't bring happiness, we need to constantly check our practice against our supposed beliefs. I had this point driven home when my wife and I spent two months working in southern Ethiopia on a church mission project. As newlyweds we thought we had a pretty modest lifestyle, but our opinions changed as we worked with people who were focused on providing only the most basic needs for their families. Suddenly Glenda and I were the rich people who were offered deferential treatment as the church's guests. We learned that "rich" is a relative term, and that summer we had our definition of "enough" radically challenged. We experienced the unintended negative consequences of deferential treatment. It was a lesson that changed how we treated money—and those who had more than we did—after we returned home. One of the greatest things about the gospel is its ability to flatten man-made hierarchies. Yet despite the equalizing power of the gospel, we too often revert to placing people on pedestals because of their money, position, education, or a host of other things. James reminds us that our choice to honor one person can lead to dishonoring another. How much worse is it, then, if the person we choose to honor is unworthy, as in James' example of the rich dragging believers off to court.

Money is amoral; it is neither good nor evil. Ecclesiastes offers a useful perspective about both ends of the spectrum regarding wealth. Having an abundance is a blessing from God, especially the ability to enjoy it (see Eccl 5:18–20). We should enjoying the fruit of our labor as a gift from God! But there is also a darker side to money, especially an abundance of it, described in Ecclesiastes 5:10–12:

> Whoever loves money is not satisfied with money,
>   and whoever loves wealth is not satisfied with profit.
> This also is vanity!
> When prosperity increases,
>   those who consume it increase.
> So its owner gains nothing,
>   except to see his wealth before it is spent.

> The sleep of the laborer is pleasant, whether he eats little or much,
> but the wealth of the rich man does not allow him to rest.

Although money might relieve certain pressures, it quite often increases pressure in other areas. Wealth can cause an abundance of worry and stress if our goal is maintaining and protecting. Paul reminds us in 1 Timothy 6:10 that it is the *love* of money that is the root of all sorts of evil, not the money itself. God has entrusted each of us with varying amounts; it is his, not ours. When we act as owners rather than stewards, things can get ugly in a hurry.

Our faith and source of boasting can shift from the Creator to the created; one is eternal, the other is fleeting. James reminds us that those who rely on wealth alone will find their boasting as short lived as a flower under the scorching sun. The blooming stage of grasses is a passing thing—flowers do not last. Similarly disasters, bad investments, and unforeseen circumstances can have the same destructive effects on wealth, no matter how much we might have. The key questions we must ask ourselves are these: What are we investing in? What is it that drives us? Is it our passion and love for God, or our passion and love for material possession and gain?

Based on this apparent human tendency to esteem those with wealth, another question to consider is what we doing with what we have. Are we showing it off to gain honor and esteem? Are we using it as a substitute for depth of character and relationship with God? Or to put it in James' terms, are we a blooming flower about to be scorched? Money is neither good nor evil—it is what we do with what we have that matters.

James 1:12–18

In this section James returns to the opening idea about considering trials "all joy." James portrays the preceding sections about wisdom (verses 5–6) and boasting (verses 9–11) in Greek as distinct points that build on his opening exhortation in verses 2–4. He uses no explicit connecting word to introduce verse 12, so he establishes his return to his earlier theme by using verbal repetition. James is not resuming the same line of development but is taking the topic of testing and endurance in a new direction.

In his first look at trials in verses 2–4, James exhorted us to consider them joy rather than hardship or punishment, based on their positive effects: maturity and lacking in nothing. James adds in verse 12 that the one who endures trials is blessed. Why? There is something more tangible than maturity that awaits us down the road: the crown of life.

So what exactly does James mean here by the crown of life? Is it something that only the uber-righteous ones who endure trials receive, or is it something else? It is important to step back here and consider James' style of argumentation, which can be a little unsettling. In fact, it led Martin Luther to argue against including the book of James in the New Testament. In a number of places, James makes his argument by calling basic assumptions into question. This is especially the case in the section on faith versus works (2:14–26). James' strategy for exhorting us to action—in this case, to endure testing and trials—is to remind us of the bigger eternal picture. It is easy to get distracted by the here and now, to forget about the reward that awaits us when Christ returns and all things are set in order. For those who love God, one of those rewards is a crown of life. James is not introducing new incentives to encourage us to obey. Instead he reminds us of what we have already been promised. But when he describes these things, he makes it sound as though the reward is only for the ones who do X instead of for all believers. This is why verse 12 reads as if only a subgroup of believers will receive the crown of life. Let's take a closer look at what he says—and what he does *not* say.

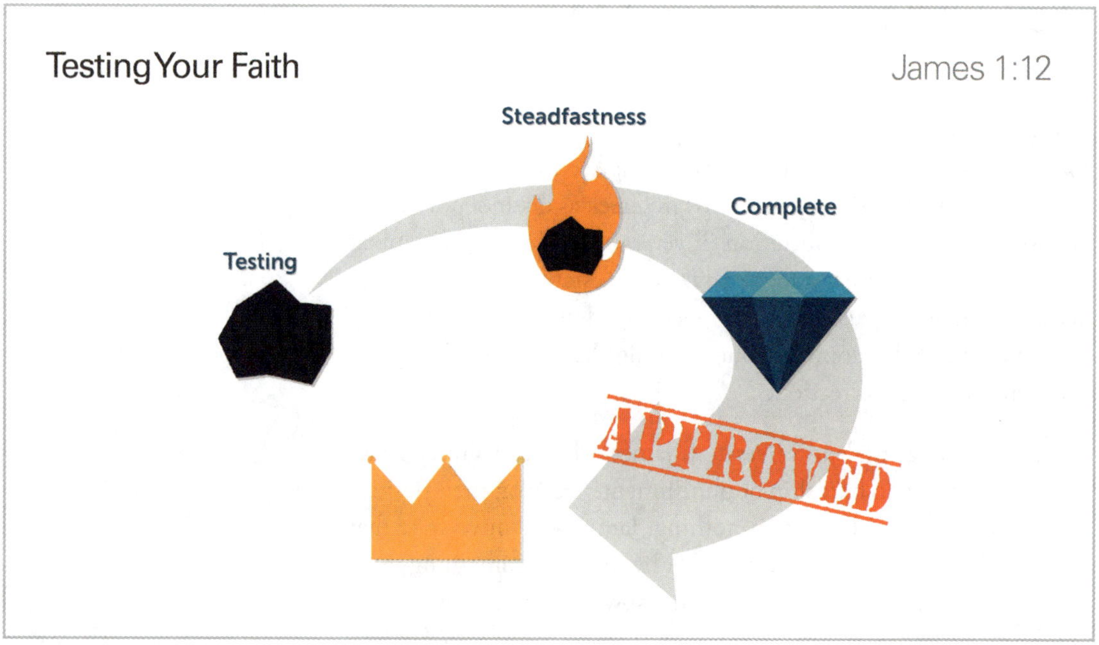

Testing Your Faith: James resumes the topic of enduring trials to add a further comment about what those who endure the testing of their faith can expect. In addition to gaining endurance and being made complete, the ones approved can look forward to receiving the crown of life.

First: What does James mean by "crown of life"? We find this phrase in Revelation 2:10 describing the same kind of reward being given in response to faithful perseverance, even to the point of death. It is quite likely that both of these mentions refer to eternal life spent with God, the life *after* physical death. This view is consistent with James' description of this crown being *promised* to those who love God. This means it is not something that can be taken away or lost.

Now, let's return to the original question about who receives the crown. Is it just for the super-righteous whose faith never flinches during trials, or does the promise apply to "those who love God" like the verse says? The qualification that James adds makes clear that the crown of life has been promised to those who love God, not just those who persevere under trial. So why would he make it sound as if it is only for those who are unflinching under trial? Part of James' rhetorical strategy is to convince readers of the importance of this action. By implying that only those who persevere will receive a crown, James compels us to strive to be one of those unflinching folks. What if he had said, "You'll get a crown either way, but it would be better if you persevered under trial"? I, at least, would be much more inclined to just rest on the promises instead of doing the tough work of persevering.

The way James frames his statement in verse 12 transforms what we have already been promised into an incentive to go "all in" and pursue the crown of life. But hasn't it been promised? Yes. So does God break his promises? No. So why not sit back and coast, why not just get by and take the easy way out when trials come? This is precisely the attitude James wants to combat by wording his argument in this way. Think about it. He never says that those who love God but don't endure to the end will *not* receive the crown of life—he merely creates an implication in the context. It is a rhetorical move to suit his goal.

What is James' goal here? To spur on his audience to faithfully follow God, even in the midst of life's adversity. This passage is not teaching about who will or will not receive a crown of life. Rather, James focuses our attention on the prize that has been promised to those of us who love God. Yes, his phrasing creates the impression that this crown might be in jeopardy if we don't endure. However, we must factor his additional description about the crown being promised into our understanding. As we will see, James uses the same jarring strategy in his comparison of faith and works in James 2:14–16.

By returning to the topic of trials and endurance in verse 12, James creates an opportunity to tackle a thorny issue: the notion that God is somehow responsible for the temptations we face. How does temptation relate to trials? The Greek noun for "trials" in verse 2 is the same word in verse 12, derived from the same root as the verb "tempt," used four times in verses 13–14. This word can refer to general testing or more specifically to moral testing (i.e., temptation).

Remember that James clarifies the *nature* of the trials in verse 2 by reframing it in verse 3 as a testing of one's faith, typically things that we can't control. He provides the same kind of clarification here in verse 13, but the trials are no longer tests of faith stemming from a force or thing beyond our control (e.g., a cancer diagnosis or an economic downturn). Here, the temptations that he has in mind concern our giving in to evil—something completely under our control. This second kind of trial includes the kind that we bring on ourselves when we give in to our evil, sinful inclinations. How can we be sure of this? James offers two reasons that feature an important qualification, indicated by italics. In the second half of the verse, James states that God cannot be tempted *by evil*, nor does he himself tempt anyone. By including this qualification "by evil" in verse 13, James makes clear that testing by amoral forces is no longer his focus, but rather temptation of our morals, testing our ability to choose not do evil.

From God?: Where does the moral testing we face actually come from? Are these tests sent from God in the same way that trials are—are they another way to test our faith? James wholeheartedly says, "No!"

From God?

James 1:13

But why does James suggest in verse 13 that God is the one who should be held responsible for temptations we face? After all, it seems people are more inclined to agree with Flip Wilson, who made popular the claim that "the Devil made me do it!" When James puts God in the crosshairs as the potential origin of moral temptation, he is following in a long history of blaming God, beginning with Adam in the garden of Eden back in Genesis 3:12. In response to God's question about eating fruit from the forbidden tree, Adam responds, "The woman whom you gave to be with me—she gave to me from the tree and I ate." In other words, Adam implies that it was really God's fault, as though none of this would have happened if God hadn't created that woman. Adam's excuse presupposes that God is the one to blame for his own sinful decisions. Blaming God for moral temptations we face is nothing new.

Since we all face temptation, we must understand its origins to effectively combat it. If moral temptations really do come from God, then we are hapless victims since God is sovereignly in control of all things. We could appeal to Paul's hypothetical complaint from Romans 9:19 that we are powerless to resist and therefore not responsible, right? Only if God really is the source of moral temptation, which James makes clear he isn't.

So where does temptation come from if not from God? To answer this question, James turns to an ugly truth—one we too often overlook. Not all trials originate from outside sources. James points out that we bring some trials on ourselves through our own bad decisions. So instead of pointing the finger at God (or the devil) as the source of all our immoral desires, James says we need to consider our own responsibility in the matter. Are our evil desires the real root of the problem?

To help us understand how our desires operate, James personifies them as a pied piper, dragging and enticing us away, luring us to follow along and give in. The process that James describes in verses 14–15 has huge implications for how we conceptualize and combat sin. Why? Just think about how we talk about sin. We talk about "falling into sin" or committing a sin, depicting sin as though it is an *event*—something that just happens all of a sudden—rather than as a multistep *process*. Recognizing this distinction has huge implications for how we combat our sinful desires!

From God?

James 1:14

From God?: After eliminating the possibility that God is the source of our temptation to sin, James redirects us to consider the role our own desires play. He portrays temptation as a process rather than an event. In doing so, he helps us recognize the ways of escape available to us to avoid giving into our sinful desires.

The first battle in the war against sin is with the evil desires that try to entice us and drag us away. Our response? We must turn away from these desires and not give in to them. In and of themselves, the desires are not sinful; instead, our choice to dwell on and feed them causes the problem. Paul paints a picture of this in Romans 7:7–12 in describing how knowledge of the law affected him. Instead of quelling his desires, knowledge of the law magnified his desire to rebel.

So how should we respond? Paul spells it out in Romans 6:12–14: "Therefore do not let sin reign in your mortal body, so that you obey its desires, and do not present your members to sin as instruments of unrighteousness, but present yourselves to God as those who are alive from the dead, and your members to God as instruments of righteousness. For sin will not be master over you, because you are not under law, but under grace." Paul also provides guidance about the important role the Spirit plays in this process in Romans 8:4–11. But for James, the focus here for is on the source of temptation. Instead of blaming God—as if we are powerless in the midst of temptation—James counters by demonstrating the pivotal role of our desires in the process.

So what happens if we lose the first battle and give in to the desires? What if we allow ourselves to be dragged away? In verse 15, James declares it means we have given birth to a bouncing baby sin. Now instead of just facing a desire, we must do battle with its offspring—sin. We face a second battle, a critical choice: Do we care for it and nurture it, providing everything it needs to grow and mature? If we do, then there is only one outcome we should expect: death. And it won't be the sin that dies—it will be us! It will destroy our relationship with God and with those around us.

Why does James go into such detail depicting sin as a process? Because this knowledge better enables us to understand our enemy. Temptations do not come from God, so we need to drop that belief immediately. Rather, they arise from our own desires. This would still be true even if the devil were involved; he appeals to our desires. Our first line of defense is to recognize this and combat the desires before the battle is lost. James offers practical help for this in verses 19–20.

And if we should give in to our desires and sin as a result, what then? We should repent, turning away from what we've done instead of continuing down that path. But the important thing to recognize is that the battle is won or lost when we choose how to respond to the call of our desires. The realization that *I,* not God, am the one to blame for giving in to moral temptation eliminates any possibility of claiming to be a victim of something beyond my control. Remember Adam tried blaming his sinful decision on the woman God had given him. The crux of the battle against temptation is to accept that it all originates with our sinful desires.

Another important distinction to be made here is that not all trials are "created equal," so to speak. Some trials come into our lives that are truly beyond our control. These stand in contrast to trials that we bring on ourselves: natural consequences of our own sinful decisions. In most cases, our sin comes with natural, typically negative, consequences. Our response—to resist or give in—to that initial enticement can affect the number and severity of trials we face. So instead of verse 14 referring to generic trials that test and build our faith as in verses 2–4, James portrays this subset of trials as natural consequences of giving in to our immoral desires.

God may bring tests into our lives that build our faith, but we can be assured that he will never tempt us with evil. It turns out we don't really need any help in that area; our sinful desires do a pretty good job by themselves.

But there is another aspect of the moral battle against sin that we cannot overlook—one James tackles in verses 14b–15: the myth of "falling" into sin. This common characterization of the process makes it sound like sin just happens, as if we tripped on the stairs or fell off a cliff. This belief makes sin an event, but James is clear that sin is a process. Our desires do more than just tempt us; they will entice us and drag us away *if* we give in to them. Temptations are all around us. We are dragged away only *after* we give in to them, not before. If we can recognize that sin is a process, we will be in a much better position to recognize the off-ramps God provides for us to escape (see 1 Cor 10:13).

So what will we do when temptations come? What James describes in verse 15 might be likened to incubating the desires, giving them what they need so that they can grow up to be big and strong. We must acknowledge our role in the process and starve the evil desires of what they need to thrive and grow: our love and energy! James makes clear that we must focus our attention here, abandoning the lie that sin just happens, that we fall into sin without warning.

In verse 16, James returns to the topic he set aside in verse 13: God. Instead of describing what God does *not* do, James offers a positive alternative by describing what he *does* do. The negative part from verse 13 serves as a foil against which to highlight that our desires are the real problem. But this shift away from God to our desires left things on a negative note that James addresses here.

Verses 16–17 form one complex thought, with verse 16 serving as an attention-getter for the big idea introduced in verse 17. The combination of the unneeded form of address ("my dear brothers") and the command ("do not be deceived") mark a shift in the discourse, the kind normally associated with the beginning of a new section. However, we are still in the middle of the section, approaching a climactic statement. When a writer uses a transitional device at a point where there is no major transition, it has the effect of attracting extra attention to what immediately follows. It would be similar to someone prefacing an important statement with, "Now don't miss this, people." This preamble statement does not move the discussion forward, but rather comments on what is about to be said.

God is a powerful source, but not of the temptations dismissed in verse 13. James highlights his transition to the correct view by using the exhortation, "Do not be deceived, my beloved brothers." This unnecessary metacomment directs our attention to what immediately follows: God is the source of every good and perfect gift, not the temptations that we face. James' declaration connects back to verses 5–6 and his exhortation to ask God for wisdom if we lack it. In verses 16–17, he adds that there is a lot more good stuff where wisdom comes from—every manner of good and perfect gift.

James has phrased his comments to highlight the source of the gifts. His statement presupposes the *existence* of every good and perfect gift; he wants his readers to learn *where* they come from. This parallels his earlier reference to God and temptations in verse 13. James presupposes that they, too, exist—it is just a matter of their source. In verse 17, he uses emphasis in Greek to highlight the source: from above, implying they have heavenly origins.

From God!: In the preceding verses, James has already explained that God is not the source of our temptation—the source is our sinful desires. But God is a powerful source: James tells us that every good and perfect gift from above comes from him. He is called "the Father of lights," in contrast to Satan or our own dark desires.

The balance of verse 17 elaborates on the one main idea about the source of all good and perfect gifts. James doesn't say they originate with God, but rather from "the Father of lights." This recharacterization of God sets the stage for James to use the light metaphor to comment on the unchanging nature of God's character. Lights can grow and fade in intensity, and James is able to leverage this knowledge to help his readers better understand the unvarying nature of our heavenly Father.

James also used the light metaphor to contrast changing shadows with God's unchanging character. As lights—or things that cast shadows—move about, so do the shadows that are cast. We have all seen changing shadows under a tree as the wind blows through it on a sunny day, constantly changing the patterns of light. Although shifting shadows can be pretty, they can also ruin the usefulness of the light. Walking with a candle or a flashlight is very different than walking on a naturally lit path. The movement of the shifting shadows can distract us from where we should be looking. Sometimes the movement can be downright spooky. We can't know precisely why James chose this metaphor, but first-century readers would have been very familiar with the challenges of poor lighting and shifting shadows. Casting God as an unwavering source of light, one that does not shift or change, provides a powerful image of his character.

James 1:19–27

James gets our attention and shifts gears to a new topic with the exhortation "understand" in verse 19. This expression is used only a handful of times in the New Testament (Eph 5:5; Heb 12:17). In each case what follows is not so much a new topic, but rather an important piece of information that informs the preceding discussion. James combines this attention-getting exhortation with the unneeded direct address "my dear brothers"—much like he does in verse 16—to highlight the comment that immediately follows. But whereas the highlighted comment in verse 16 resumes the earlier topic of what God provides, the exhortations that follow here in verse 19 introduce the big idea for the section that follows. In Greek there is no explicit connecting word to let us know whether this is a new point or one building on what precedes. James leaves it to the reader to make that decision.

He begins this section with a command to be quick to hear, slow to speak, and slow to anger. He phrases these as one complex command rather than as three separate ones. He also uses a less-direct approach, more of a request than a command. He could have addressed the audience more directly by saying, "(You) be quick to listen, be slow to speak, be slow to anger." By addressing "everyone" instead of "you," James effectively softens the nature of the exhortation.

So why should we be quick to hear, slow to speak, and slow to anger? James offers an answer in verse 20, contrasting human anger with divine righteousness. The implication? That our human propensity to be quick to speak and quick to anger does not originate from God's righteousness, but from our giving in to our desires to vent our frustration and anger (see verse 14). With this contrast of anger with righteousness, James quashes the possibility of justifying our outbursts of anger or rudeness. If we really are seeking after God's righteousness, then venting through our speech and emotional outbursts is not the way to go about it. Rather, the key is to slow down these responses and patiently listen.

Quick or Slow? James 1:19

Quick or Slow?: There is not a one-size-fits-all solution when it comes to how we interact with other people. James commands us to do the opposite of what is natural for many of us. When something upsets us, our inclination is much more likely to be to speak or get angry rather than to listen. The big question is this: What are we characterized by? Am I quick to react and slow to listen? What do my communication gauges read most of the time? We must step on the brakes when it comes to speaking and getting angry, giving the right of way to listening.

Being quicker to hear would likely solve many of the disagreements we face in life. I remember as a new believer learning about how best to confront sin issues, as described in Matthew 18:15–20. The instructions that Jesus offers are consistent with James' exhortation to slow our anger and be quicker to listen. The first step is to go and talk to the other person alone and try to work it out. I learned that there are essentially three possible outcomes from this first step. I could be missing some information, the other person could be missing some information, or there could actually be a disagreement.

Let's say I went to confront someone about how they had mistreated me one day; say that it had offended me, and I wanted them to ask me forgiveness. I have learned that when offensive behavior is out of character for someone, then there is generally a backstory. In the majority of cases, hearing the backstory completely changes my perception of the "offense." Had I known the cause for what was happening, I never would have come to confront them in the first place. As I have grown and matured over the years, I find that I am not nearly so zealous in confronting what I feel is offensive behavior. Paul's words in Romans 12:18–21 make a lot more sense now.

But there are, nevertheless, times where someone has done something out of line that warrants attention. After listening and hearing them out, another possible outcome is learning that *they* are the ones missing a piece of needed information. In other words, the offense was not so much intentional as it was inadvertent. They didn't know any better. A great example of this is found in Acts 18:24–28, where Priscilla and Aquila pulled Apollos aside and "explained the way of God to him more accurately." I doubt there was any yelling involved; it was likely more of a redirection. What Apollos needed was not a tongue lashing but the information he was missing in order to teach more accurately. Jesus says that if the one you are correcting listens to you, you have won your brother (Matt 18:15). In other words, the goal is winning your brother, not winning the argument. Too often, this goal can get lost in the heat of the moment.

The last potential outcome is that both of us have accurately heard each other, but we still disagree over what is right or what should be done. In my personal experience, this last category is the least frequent. If there really is a disagreement, then James' exhortation to be quick to listen, slow to speak, and slow to anger is all the more critical to having a constructive outcome. If a person sees you are quicker to listen than to speak, you have a much better chance of establishing the trust and rapport needed to resolve the disagreement. Remember, the goal is not to win the argument, but to win your brother or sister.

In verse 21, James resumes the main idea of verse 19, which was interrupted by the strengthening material of verse 20. So what are we supposed to do, based on the fact that our anger doesn't accomplish the righteousness of God? What does it take to be quick to hear and slow to speak or get angry? James outlines two steps. The first requires that we lay aside the moral uncleanness and excessive wickedness that would likely lead to impatience and speaking out to vent our anger. In Greek this first step is backgrounded, making the second step stand out as more important. Both are needed, but James places a higher priority on the second.

Getting the Word?: James describes how human anger doesn't accomplish the righteousness of God. He then turns to the only means that can: accepting God's Word, which is able to save our souls. He paints a contrasting picture here of those who humbly accept God's Word and allow it to be implanted within them, and those who—because of uncleanness and wicked excess—are unwilling to accept it. The same word that is humbly implanted in the one is completely ineffective in the other.

What is this second step? Welcoming what James calls "the implanted message." What kind of message are we welcoming? The kind that can save our souls. Say what? James is a theological provocateur, wording things so as to rattle our cages and get us to pay attention. This information about the message's ability to save our souls recharacterizes it by making it sound like there might be some other implanted message we might welcome. The extra description influences the importance we assign it. If a message is significant enough to save your soul, wouldn't you make it a priority to welcome it? You bet! This says nothing about whether someone has already accepted the message that will save their soul; it merely assigns a value and importance to that message.

But wait, there's more! James also specifies the manner in which we are to receive this soul-saving, implanted message: with humility. James even uses emphasis in Greek to drive home the point. The emphasis causes us to contrast receiving it with humility versus receiving it some other possible way. Calling it the "implanted word" reinforces the notion of receiving it, in the sense that it is there to stay.

James shifts to a new point in verse 22 that builds on this exhortation to humbly receive the implanted word. Even though the Word is powerful enough to save one's soul, James expects us to do something more than just passively receive the word. He challenges us to be *doers* of this word, not just hearers of it. James goes on to say that if we think that hearing the word is what matters, rather than doing it, we are deceiving ourselves. This is the same kind of message we find in Micah 6:8: God is not just concerned with us having the right knowledge, but rather rightly acting on that knowledge by doing justice, loving kindness, and walking humbly before God.

So why should we focus our attention on doing and not just knowing? What's the big deal? James provides a practical illustration in verses 23–25 of what hearing without doing looks like. Most of us regularly use some sort of mirror. They are great for seeing things that we can't see on our own—is our hair or tie in place, or did we drop something behind a cabinet? Mirrors are made for giving us a clear perspective of things that we would most likely not have gotten on our own. This is the backdrop for James' illustration. If I have a mirror and use it to check something but then immediately forget what I saw, then what's the point of looking in the mirror in the first place? If I don't gain a new perspective or insight from using it, then why even bother to look?

The same holds true for the implanted word. Receiving it humbly is only the beginning. James drives this point home with a practical illustration. He introduces a person by creating a specific scenario—someone being a hearer of the word and not a doer. The near-verbatim repetition of this idea from verse 22 leaves no room for missing James' point. All too often we focus our energy on simply acquiring more knowledge without striving to apply it. Why? It's easy to believe that I need just a bit more knowledge before I really know enough to make a difference; it's easy to tell ourselves, "Of course I'm going to apply what I've learned, just as soon as I've learned it a bit better." Have you ever caught yourself saying something similar?

James tells us this idea is equivalent to having a mirror and never using it properly. Oh, sure, you look into it from time to time, but if you never act on the knowledge it reflects, then what's the point of having the mirror?

Hearer vs. Doer

James 1:23–25

Hearer vs. Doer: Mirrors provide us a chance to see things that we otherwise might miss. The key question is what we will do with this knowledge. This is the dilemma James uses to make his point. He portrays the "perfect law of liberty" as something that reveals imperfections in us. We have two choices of how to respond. Either we act on the knowledge we gain from what we see, or we walk away and forget we ever saw anything in the first place. This is the difference between hearing and doing versus hearing and *not* doing.

James tackles this issue even more bluntly in 2:14–17, concluding that faith by itself—without works—is dead. Ouch! We are a society that highly values knowledge for its own sake, but James challenges us to reconsider. From his standpoint, God has implanted this knowledge in us for one reason: to act on it.

James offers a positive picture in verse 25 to contrast with the forgetful hearer. He also redefines the mirror as the perfect law of liberty, something that can set us free instead of box us in. The key difference with this second person is what happens after they walk away from the mirror. They don't just look at the law and forget; they persevere in what they have seen. What exactly does this entail? James explains that it means not being a forgetful hearer, but rather a doer, one who acts. And what can this doer expect? To be blessed, not in their knowledge, but in their *doing*.

I don't know about you, but James' words make me pretty uncomfortable. I like to think that "it's the thought that counts." Knowledge is powerful in and of itself, right? Yes, but we must keep in mind that James isn't devaluing the importance of having knowledge; in fact, he *presupposes* you have it. Remember his exhortation to ask for wisdom if you are lacking it (1:5)? So knowledge is not the problem, but James has absolutely no patience for those who fail to act on the knowledge they have obtained. Hearing these words strips away any excuse for not acting on what we have learned. More knowledge might help, but we need to be faithful in acting on what we already know. Otherwise we can become puffed up by our knowledge, even letting knowledge become an end rather than a means to an end.

The last verses in this chapter consider a practical example of what James means by hearing and doing versus just hearing. Once again, he introduces a state of affairs using a conditional statement: "If anyone does A and B, then C applies." He mentions all three of these things in verse 26. Just as he makes an important distinction between hearing and doing, he distinguishes between what he calls "pure and undefiled religion" in verse 27. The first part of verse 26 introduces the A and B that establish the situation. A is considering yourself to be religious. B consists of two parts: not bridling your tongue and deceiving yourself. The phrasing of the Greek pits bridling the tongue against deceiving yourself, as though you are either doing one or the other if you think you are religious. You can't think you are religious and not bridle your tongue; otherwise you are deceiving yourself. But this is not James' main point—it is just the setup for what's coming.

James brings together these contrasting elements of religion—bridling and deception—from the first part of the verse to comment on them in the second. If people don't bridle their tongues, if they deceive themselves, then how should we look on their religion? How does it measure up? James tells us that it is worthless and explains the correlation he draws between not bridling the tongue and deceiving oneself. He shifts from a simple distinction between hearing and doing to a more specific consideration of how things are done, or perhaps which things take precedence over others. He sharply contrasts a person's own perception of religiosity with how God evaluates such matters. The way James phrases verse 27 drives this point home.

What's it Worth? James 1:26–27

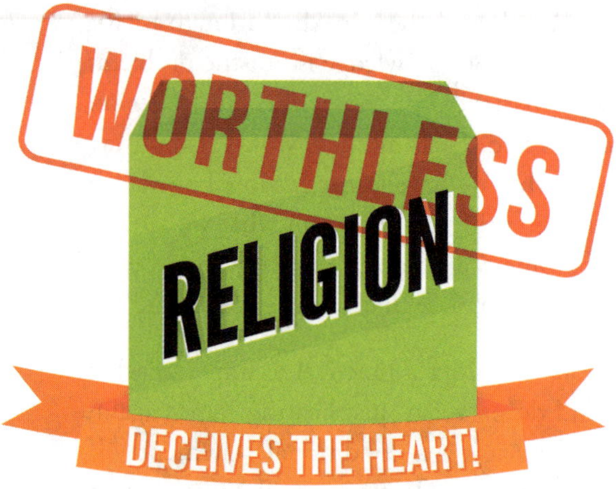

What's it Worth?: What exactly is it that makes someone's religious practices worthwhile? James answers this question by assessing the value of someone claiming to be religious without having the self-control to bridle their tongue. How does it measure up? It's worthless! Rather than being commendable, such religion actually deceives the person's heart. James contrasts such religion with that of a person who cares for the needs of orphans and widows—such religion is pure and undefiled.

James begins by introducing religion that is pure and undefiled. No longer can we be the determiners of what is religious and what is not. The basis for determining the "pure and undefiled" qualities is our God and Father's sight rather than our own. To draw extra attention to how this religion looks in practice, James uses a forward-pointing reference—"pure and undefiled religion is *this*..."—where "this" refers ahead to the important point James makes. What counts in God's sight is looking after widows and orphans and keeping oneself unstained by the world.

James also includes details that remind us about the plight of widows and orphans, calling attention to their misfortune or distress. You see, in the Old Testament law, God singled out certain kinds of people within the nation of Israel who deserved special care and attention (Exod 22:22). Each is identified by a lack of something that most others have: Widows lack a husband; orphans lack parents; foreigners/aliens lack a landed inheritance; the poor lack money. God singled out these four kinds of people for special consideration in the law. In fact, God even promised that he would take up their cause to see that they found justice (Deut 10:18). In other words, if you took advantage of a widow or orphan, God himself would hold you accountable. By referring back to the two quintessential members of these groups—widows and orphans—and the adversity that most of them face, James evokes the Old Testament teachings about how an upstanding, religious Israelite was to look after such people (Deut 24:17–22).

Sometimes our rationale for what impresses God doesn't match the standards he has outlined. But why would we want to develop our own standards? To begin with, creating our own makes it much easier to earn high marks! We might build our standards based on things we think would please God, or we might use how others see us as that standard. This is easier to do than you might think. Over the years I have allowed praise of my teaching to serve as a poor substitute for God's perspective on my life. While the teaching may well have been God-honoring, he has much more in store to continue growing me into maturity. But if I gravitate toward what comes naturally, what I am praised for, and exclude the things I find challenging or unpleasant, haven't I created my own standards of religiosity? What fits my definition of healthy might very well be stunting my spiritual growth! It's like eating an unbalanced diet. If we avoid the healthy things that challenge us to spiritual maturity—eating our proverbial vegetables—what will be the result? This is where serving others, especially the most vulnerable, can play such a vital role in balancing our spiritual growth.

Knowledge is important, but it's not enough in and of itself. James makes clear that acting on what we have heard is what matters, not just hearing it. What is meaningful to God, what really counts in his eyes? Looking after the marginalized, who have always been dear to him. We need to make sure our priorities match up with his.

The other aspect of God-pleasing behavior that James mentions is keeping oneself "unstained by the world." Last I checked, there's no spiritual equivalent to the kind of stain-guard coatings applied to clothing or carpets. This means instead of just playing through when spills occur, Christians must avoid the situations that would stain us in the first place. Elsewhere, Paul reminds us that completely withdrawing from this world is not a viable option unless we literally leave the planet (1 Cor 5:9–10). The choice we face every day and every hour is how we respond to the influences around us. When we embrace and cozy up to them, we're very likely to get stained.

Allowing God's implanted Word and freely given wisdom to shape us and to guard our hearts and minds is the very best way we can avoid those staining influences.

James 2

James 2:1–13

James signals the shift to a new topic through the use of redundant address ("my brothers") and an exhortation not to hold our faith with partiality. What does this mean on a practical level? James uses a very complex set of "if" conditions that stretches all the way through the end of verse 4 to make one important "then" statement. These conditions evoke a vivid scenario that he uses to critique the entirety of the situation. He accomplishes the same task as that we do when we say, "Let's suppose that someone enters your assembly in fine clothing, and you look favorably on the one…" The conditions do not mean that this exact scenario must occur before we make a favorable distinction; it is simply a common strategy in Greek for signaling a hypothetical situation.

What does the scenario entail? Believers treating a rich person and a poor person differently purely on the basis of their appearance, in the context of a church meeting of some kind. The rich one is ushered to a favorable spot, whereas the poor one is either to stand or sit in an unfavorable spot. After introducing the scenario, James asks a question that draws out his point: If believers adjust their behavior or response to someone based on their status or outward appearance, aren't they making distinctions?

Two Views of the Poor

James 2:1–5

Two Views of the Poor: Our treatment of people can be prejudiced at times by their outward appearances, what James calls "making distinctions." In his scenario, those who look like they might have something to offer us are given preferential treatment, whereas those with little to offer are disrespected or mistreated. To address this problem of making distinctions, James contrasts our human perspective and God's divine perspective. The poor person we think has little to offer is—from God's standpoint—an heir of the kingdom and rich in faith. Appearances can be misleading, so we must adopt God's point of view in how we treat people.

So are all distinctions wrong? James adds a clarifying comment later in verse 4. If we make this kind of distinction, we are essentially a judge with evil thoughts. Think about that for a minute. Why *would* anyone want to make a distinction between the rich and the poor? There might be many specific reasons, but the one James seems to have in mind is their ability to do something in return for us. Jesus tackles the same issue in Luke 6:31–34:

> And just as you want people to do to you, do the same to them. And if you love those who love you, what kind of credit is that to you? For even sinners love those who love them! And if you do good to those who do good to you, what kind of credit is that to you? Even the sinners do the same! And if you lend to those from whom you expect to receive back, what kind of credit is that to you? Even sinners lend to sinners, so that they may get back an equal amount!

If we are to love our neighbor as ourselves, then there is no room for making distinctions between rich and poor. The basis of our distinctions reveals what we value and how we determine someone else's value. Do we judge others based on what they might do for us in return? Do we defer to those we think are more prestigious than us in the hopes of gaining acceptance or affirmation? Unfortunately, I sometimes need to answer "yes" on both counts. This might be how we value people from a human perspective, but James reworks the equation in verses 5–7 to show how things add up from God's perspective.

James redirects our attention from a hypothetical scenario to a reality check with "listen my dear brother" in verse 5. He reminds us that God has chosen the poor to be rich in something other than monetary wealth. Instead of extensive land holdings received from wealthy relatives, the poor hold title as heirs of God's kingdom. If we read carefully, we see that James is not saying we have to be poor to be an heir, or that all poor folks are automatically rich in faith and heirs of his kingdom. James qualifies the kingdom he has in mind as "the one that he has promised to those who love him." Gaining this inheritance is still a matter of faith, but James is again rattling our cage by casting the poor in a particular light. His point is that our prejudicial behavior dishonors the poor.

James moves on in verses 6–7 to a reality check about the rich who were given deferential treatment in the scenario he described. James has no need to appeal to divine sensibilities to describe the rich. Instead, he uses archetypal behavior to characterize the rich, as if he is reminding us of something we should already know, with the question: "Are not the rich exploiting you and they themselves dragging you into the courts?" The last part of verse 7 implies this is unscrupulous behavior since it results in blaspheming God's good name. Instead of making an explicit reference to God, James substitutes "the one to whom you belong," creating the impression that the poor belong to God, but not the rich. Again, this doesn't mean rich people can't belong to God or do good things with their money. James is using archetypes to jar our sensibilities and make us rethink our basis for how we treat people. He is correcting our predilection for misdirecting honor and respect. We must not follow the worldly tendency to value money over godliness.

Two Views of Rich

James 2:5–7

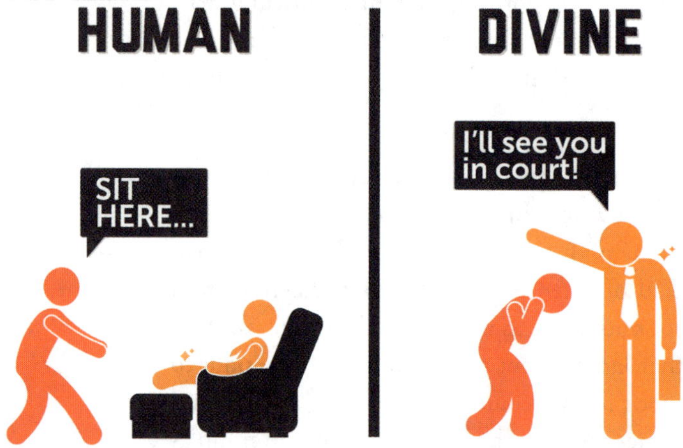

Two Views of Rich: Too often we make distinctions based on what we think another person might be able to do for us. James paints a portrait of what this might look like in a church setting. To address this problem of making distinctions, James offers a different perspective—one that clashes with our human perspective. Writing from God's divine perspective, James portrays the rich as being unfair to the average person. They are the ones who take advantage of people, dragging them into court. This is not to say that all the rich are evil and all the poor are righteous. Rather, this represents how our evil motives affect how we treat others. Appearances can be misleading, so we must adopt God's point of view in how we treat people.

In verse 8, James returns to his exhortation from verse 1 to exercise our faith without partiality. He uses another condition—a parallel to the complex one he used in verses 2–4—to create a cohesive link between the two. If holding distinctions is negative, then a positive alternative is loving our neighbors as ourselves. James characterizes this action as carrying out the royal law. He even uses emphasis to drive home the importance of keeping this law—but he structures the emphasis to serve as a rhetorical backdrop for verse 9. Although this is the desired outcome, James describes it as though it is not the expected one.

James resumes his prosecution of distinction making, emphasizing that it's not just a bad idea, it's *sin*. So instead of upholding the royal law through love, those who make distinctions are convicted by the same law as transgressors. And to any who might think that making distinctions isn't really a big deal, James nips that idea in the bud too. You see, it is not simply a matter of *mostly* keeping the law.

Whole vs. Part

James 2:10–11

Whole vs. Part: James has some harsh news for anyone who judges others' behavior without considering how they themselves will be judged: Keeping *most* of the law will not suffice in God's eyes. When we choose not to show mercy to others and yet we stumble in our own obedience to the law, we will experience the same lack of mercy from God. James challenges us to correct how we treat others by considering how our behavior will influence our judgment by God.

James unequivocally describes how such legal matters are reconciled, and it's a daunting prospect. Let's say a person kept the whole law, but stumbled in just one small aspect—what about them? James says they would be guilty of the entire law, not just the one bit they botched. James explains that the same God who forbids adultery is the same one who also forbids murder. In other words, no matter the area of law in which we fail, we still offend the same God. Offense is offense, regardless.

So how should we, as lawbreakers, respond to the prospects of divine judgment? By keeping this judgment in mind when we are tempted to judge others. In verse 12, James exhorts us to speak and to act in a particular way. He even uses an attention-getting device to make sure we don't miss what he's saying. We all fall short of perfect law-keeping, so we had better keep our imperfection in mind as we interact with others. Why? Just as we should treat others the way we would want them to treat us, James tells us that God uses a comparable equation. But instead of the standard being what we would want done, the standard is what we *actually* did (verse 13). You heard it right! For the one who did not exercise mercy, James says their judgment will be merciless. But for the one who has shown mercy, they can expect to have it returned to them.

Judgment vs. Mercy: We face a choice about how we will be judged by God in the future. According to James, the mercy we show to others will be the determining factor for the mercy we will be shown by God. Practically speaking, we determine our own future regarding mercy versus judgment. Those of us who show mercy now will be shown mercy later. Those opting for judgment now will face merciless judgment in the future.

Remember how the big idea for this section is making distinctions? James has moved us beyond distinctions between rich and poor to distinctions that hit a lot closer to home for me. I am tempted to make the same kinds of distinctions all the time, treating others one way but wanting a different kind of treatment for myself. Like what? How about venting my frustration at a customer service representative on the phone when a company hasn't treated me as I wanted? That righteous indignation seems to rise up out of nowhere, and in an instant I am lashing out for something that is likely beyond their control or, worse yet, may have been my own fault. I have friends who work in customer service—and boy, do they have some stories to tell! Rude people vent at them as though they were the root of all evil. Will I let my behavior turn into another story like that, even if I *was* wronged, or will I speak with grace and mercy?

And what happens when the roles are reversed, when someone criticizes me for something I've done to them? It's an opportunity for me to make another distinction, right? Whatever I may have done to contribute to the situation, I tend to overlook my behavior as I deflect blame onto someone or something else. James condemns this type of action, where we fail to extend the same kind of love and mercy to others that we want extended to us.

So what's the moral of the story for James? That mercy triumphs over judgment. Everyone falls short of fulfilling all aspects of God's law; this is a given. But James reminds us that we can expect to face judgment as transgressors if we judge others by the same laws we have broken. James challenges us to let the coming judgment influence how we treat others *now*. His closing thought in verse 13 offers us hope: "Mercy triumphs over judgment." And based on the magnitude of mercy that God has displayed to us through new life in Christ Jesus, the least we can do is extend this same mercy to others. What we do today, James reminds us, will influence our treatment tomorrow. We should live in such a way that this is not a scary thought.

James 2:14–26

James introduces the next big idea using a rhetorical question ("What good is it…") in verse 14. His question draws our attention to the key thought for what follows. He begins by asking what the point of something is, but then he delays telling us exactly what that is by inserting "my brothers." This expression does not signal a shift to a new audience or subaudience; instead, this delay highlights James' introduction to the topic of having faith without works. In Greek, emphasis is used to highlight contrast—in this case, the contrast between faith and works.

James also offers an unnerving follow-up question at the end of verse 14—one that anticipates a negative answer. His question calls into doubt whether such a faith could save someone. Warning: We need to pay close attention to what James *actually* says and not mistake it for what he does *not* say. The focus here is not disputing whether faith is the basis of salvation. Instead, just as James contrasted the merits of hearing versus doing, he contrasts the value of faith alone versus faith that manifests itself in works. And just as James argued that hearing should lead to doing (1:22–25), he posits that faith—if it really exists—should lead to an outward expression: works. From the outset James shakes us by implying that a workless faith may not be a saving faith. This is only an *implication* of his wording, but it has caused no shortage of heartburn for theologians over the years.

Evidence of Faith

James 2:14

Evidence of Faith: How is it possible for others to see whether you have faith or to see the quality of that faith? Since faith is not tangible in itself, the only real way faith can be verified is by seeing it in action. Sure, we can claim to have faith, but James rightly questions whether faith that is never seen is really the kind of faith that can save us. Later, in verse 18, he challenges those claiming to have faith to prove it to him without any works to demonstrate it. Putting faith into action gives others a chance to see and test its quality.

In verse 15, James offers a practical illustration of the difference he sees between applied faith and a claim of faith that never manifests itself in works. His scenario introduces people who are most likely believers, based on his use of "brother or sister." These family terms imply kinship of some kind—in this case, membership in the family of God. The people are defined by what they lack: adequate clothing and sufficient daily food. James shifts from generic people to potential members of the audience in verse 16 by saying "one of you." This again implies that James is focused on believers helping other believers. The key element of the scenario is whether believers are helping others in need. Instead of offering them something from their own goods or helping them find provision elsewhere, these people are simply offering a blessing, with no practical assistance.

James delivers his carefully worded verdict regarding this kind of faith. His wording is deliberate, so we should be careful not to read too much into it; James is not staging a faith-versus-works smackdown. He highlights his key point about faith in this verse. First, there is a condition: "if it does not have works." This makes clear that faith is still a necessary component of salvation, one that cannot simply be replaced by works. Then, at the end of the verse, he adds, "by itself." This again drives home the point that faith must be put into practice, just like hearing must be accompanied by doing (see Jas 1:22–25). And what can we say about this kind of faith that is not practiced? It is dead, James says. He even shifts the order of the words to emphasize "dead" in Greek so there is no missing his point.

Warmed + Filled: To illustrate the emptiness of a faith without works, James hypothesizes a scenario where a brother or sister in Christ is in need, but a believer offers only a blessing instead of something practical that would help meet their need. While this might technically qualify as faith, James says that faith is dead unless it is accompanied by works.

You might think James has built a pretty airtight case to win his argument. But he takes it one step further, anticipating a potential objection in verse 18. It is essentially a "Yes, but …" objection to his initial point in verse 14 about the futility of someone saying they have faith but not works. I can almost hear the objection: "You just don't understand. *I* have faith, but *you* have works. Each part of the body is different, right, each fulfilling its unique role?" Again, James places emphasis on faith and works to highlight the contrast.

How does James respond to this objection? By highlighting the emptiness of the claim, challenging them to show him their faith without using works to do it. Meanwhile, James shows them his faith by taking actions that demonstrate and exercise his faith. Faith is one of many abstract things that we can't see. We talk about "having" or "possessing" these things, but they can't be seen unless they are "exercised" or "applied." For instance, I could say that I have compassion, or that I have good ideas, creativity, or even anger-management issues! You could take my word for it, but it's more likely you would look for evidence of these traits in how I live. This would require me to *do* something to show you. If intangible concepts—like compassion and faith—are not put into practice, we have no proof they exist.

Problem? James 2:17–18

Problem?: Batteries are a common source of electricity in our society. It is not the battery itself that has value, but the charge that is stored in it. Figuratively speaking, it is the application of faith that provides benefit. Faith without works is just as dead and impractical as a battery without any electrical charge.

We have lots of idioms in American English that express the same sentiment that James offers in the second part of verse 18: Take "put up or shut up," or "actions speak louder than words." Missouri is the "Show Me State." "Talk is cheap" implies that actions are more difficult and therefore more valuable. When we describe people who didn't follow up on what they said, we say that they only gave "lip service." When it comes to whether a person really possesses an intangible quality, like faith, asking to see it in practice does not negate its importance or supplant the value of the practice. It is in keeping with the old Russian proverb popularized in English by President Ronald Reagan, "Trust, but verify." If someone consistently claims to have faith, yet consistently fails to demonstrate it in their life, James' challenge is fitting. Can faith that is never seen really be a saving faith? Is it really there if it is never seen? God is undoubtedly the final judge of such things, but there are no "do-overs" when we stand before the judgment seat.

In verse 19 James offers another practical implication of claiming to possess something that hasn't necessarily brought a meaningful change in someone. Consider the belief that God is one (i.e., that there is one supreme God). Such a belief is a foundational pillar for both Christians and Jews alike, an indispensible part of orthodoxy. James essentially asks whether it is the belief alone that matters, or whether something more is required. He does this by pointing out that the demons would also wholeheartedly agree with this statement, yet they still face condemnation and eternal punishment at the final judgment. So, how is having a correct belief working for them? Not so well, apparently.

We face the same kinds of challenges with other beliefs. A mentor of mine taught me an important distinction between what he called an *actual* belief/value versus a *preferred* belief/value. Preferred beliefs are those things that we think and say are important; actual beliefs or values are the ones we act on. Consider these examples: belief in prayer, evangelism, reading our Bibles regularly, spending time with family, honesty, generosity. How many of us would say these are bad things or things we don't believe in? Not too many. But if we scrutinize our lives—how we spend our time and money, our habits, and so on—what would we find? How do those things *we say* we believe in manifest themselves in our daily practice? Thinking or giving mental assent to something is a lot easier than allowing it to transform our lives. Demons believe that God is one, but it doesn't change their decision to rebel against him. The same holds true for the one who claims to have faith yet isn't willing or able to demonstrate it.

James assigns a description to the person claiming to have faith without works: foolish or senseless (verse 20). While it might be theoretically possible to have faith without works, James says such a faith is useless. As proof he offers two exemplars of faith from the Old Testament, Abraham and Rahab. James asks a rhetorical question, one that expects a positive answer, regarding the outcome of Abraham offering up his son Isaac on the altar. He even uses a theological term strongly associated with faith to describe the effect it had—justification. This story is found in Genesis 22, seven chapters *after* Abraham's belief has been credited to him as righteousness (Gen 15:6). So was Abraham somehow justified again?

Exhibition of Faith

James 2:20–25

Exhibition of Faith: James appeals to two Old Testament examples of faith to reinforce his point about the importance of putting faith into action. Despite the declaration that Abraham's faith was credited by God as righteousness, James highlights the significance of the practical outworking of faith for Abraham and Rahab. Faith for them was not a silent, mental assent, but the basis for taking great risks to obey God.

To better understand the point that James is drawing out here, we need to take a look at what Abraham is praised for just as he is about to offer up Isaac. In Genesis 22:12 the angel of the Lord forbids Abraham to stretch out his hand against his son. Why? "For now I know that you are one who fears God, since you have not withheld your son, your only child, from me." It is not that this act of faith has somehow won Abraham some superior level of justification before God. Rather, Abraham's act has made it plain for anyone to see that he is "all in." He withholds nothing from God, not even Sarah's only biological son. Offering up his son has provided incontrovertible evidence of Abraham's faith.

In verses 22–23 James makes a connection back to the faith that was credited to Abraham as righteousness in Genesis 15:6. Abraham's works show a practical application of his faith and led to a perfecting of that faith (Jas 2:22). This is the very same terminology James uses to describe the process of building our faith in 1:2–4. There the testing of faith produces endurance, which then has its perfect effect: making a believer mature and complete, lacking in nothing. The "perfect effect" in 1:4 derives from the same Greek word as the verb "perfect/complete" in 2:22.

Here in chapter 2, James is talking about the same faith-building process as in 1:2–4. This is the basis for his jarring claim in verse 24 that a person is justified by works and not by faith *alone*. By adding the caveat *alone*, James indicates that faith still plays a necessary role. But his interest is in the *quality* of the faith. The kind of faith that justifies someone before God is faith that can be seen. It is faith that is put into practice, not the useless kind that is only spoken of. James could probably picture the jaws dropping to the floor as he wrote this, which is precisely why I think he *did* write it. He is correcting the attitude that says that mental assent is sufficient, that faith doesn't need to bring about substantive change.

Next James takes up the example of Rahab—yes, *that* Rahab, the prostitute from Jericho who hides the spies in Joshua 2. When the king of Jericho asks her to turn them over to him, she claims that they have already left and sends the messengers on a wild goose chase. Then, when the coast is clear, Rahab lowers the spies over the wall and instructs them how to evade those searching for them (Josh 2:15–21). So what exactly does Rahab's act accomplish? The spies' report to Joshua doesn't describe any military vulnerability in Jericho. Instead, they report the testimony of Rahab (Josh 2:9) as if it were their own conclusion (Josh 2:24)—that Yahweh had given all the land into their hands and that all the inhabitants of the land were melting in fear before them. God himself had already promised Joshua that he would give them this land and that no one would stand before them (Josh 1:2–6). So based on the testimony of a Canaanite prostitute, were the spies finally convinced that God would do what he said? Of all the examples that James might choose, why this one? Just as Abraham was willing to risk the life of his only biological heir to demonstrate his faith, Rahab was willing to risk her own life to demonstrate her faith that God would do what she had heard he would do. Not only are she and her family spared (Josh 6:17, 23–25), but she appears in the lineage of Jesus (Matt 1:5) and is heralded elsewhere as a model of faith (Heb 11:31).

To summarize, there is nothing here in the context to indicate that James is talking about what someone must do to be saved. His sole focus is describing the quality of faith that can save. It is not an empty faith that is never seen, one that never manifests itself in action. This kind of faith he has declared to be useless (Jas 2:20) and even dead (verses 17, 26). His goal is not to overturn a doctrine of justification by faith, but to dispel the notion that faith may be thriving and yet never seen. His qualifications about faith "by itself" (verse 17) and "alone" (verse 24) make this clear. Genuine faith is tested and perfected. It can be readily seen as it is put into practice in our works. This is the kind of faith that can save, and this is the kind of faith that James wants to see in us.

James 3

James 3:1–12

How do you introduce an uncomfortable topic that folks probably don't want to hear about? One option is to dive straight in, as James does in 2:1 when he addresses the issue of partiality. He chooses a less-direct approach here in chapter 3, sneaking up on it to catch his readers unawares. He begins with the exhortation that not many should become teachers, creating the impression that teaching is his topic for the following section. But there is a more basic issue he wants to address that affects teachers—and all of us: the power of the tongue. But first, his exhortation to teachers.

A couple of important shifts take place in short order here, answering why we shouldn't all strive to become teachers. The answer is that teachers will be held to a higher standard, a stricter judgment. Now let's go back through this passage more carefully and look at the shifts. James begins by directly addressing his audience using a plural verb ("not many of y'all should become teachers"). The plural "y'all" renders this a less-direct exhortation compared to using a singular "you," which would have individualized it. But then James shifts to include himself in the supporting statement ("*we* will receive a greater judgment"). And instead of continuing to address issues regarding teaching, James drills down on the underlying issue—how we use our speech. James' exhortation regarding teachers thus segues into broadly applicable teaching about the tongue in verses 2–4.

James begins with the general observation that we all stumble in many ways; he then reframes this idea to create a corollary—if someone *doesn't* stumble, then they are perfect or complete. In the second half of verse 2, James elaborates on what he means by "perfect." A perfect person is able to keep their whole body in check. Here comes his shift from the whole human body to the part that is most difficult to control. He transitions from the responsibility of teachers to the responsibility we all bear regarding how we use our tongues.

The illustrations of the horse and the ship James provides in verses 3–4 share a common element. Controlling one small part effectively controls the whole thing. A bit enables the rider to control the horse's actions. The same holds true for a ship's rudder, which is tiny in proportion to the overall vessel.

So how do these examples relate back to teachers facing a greater judgment and to all of us stumbling in many ways? It turns out that the human body has its own rudder-like appendage that can direct the entire being, for better or for worse. That same member effectively controls the entirety of the body, just like a bit in a horse's mouth.

James connects the dots from his illustrations back to his main argument in verse 5 with "so also/too." Although the tongue may seem small and insignificant, nevertheless the mouth can boast great things. Isn't that a good thing, though? Not necessarily. It all depends on the nature of the boast.

Remember James' comment in verse 2: We all stumble in many ways. By zeroing in on the tongue just after this, he implies that the perfect person can avoid stumbling if they keep their whole body in check. How? Well if the tongue really does direct the rest of the body, then we should focus on controlling it. James personifies the tongue, making it sound as though it alone directs our speech—not our brains, thoughts, emotions, or heart. He uses contrasting emphasis in Greek to highlight *how great* a forest is set ablaze by *how small* a flame. His thoughts about the power of the tongue echo what we find in Proverbs 12:18–19 and 21:23. Instead of quibbling over whether the tongue acts of its own accord, we had better pay close attention to these important lessons about the effects of our speech.

James' warning about the tongue is more critical today than ever. Now instead of just needing to control our speech with those around us, we must also watch our "electronic" tongue. The anonymity of the Internet has brought with it harsher forms of rhetoric than those used in interpersonal dialogue. The impersonal nature of email and online posting makes it easier to write things we would likely never say to a person standing in front of us. Add to this the lack of gestures, intonation, and other nonverbal cues, and electronic communication clearly holds much more potential for miscommunication and misunderstanding than speaking in person—and leads to the same kind of devastating outcome. Controlling our speech—in whatever form it takes—will significantly impact our relationship with others. We must heed James' warning not to allow it to burn and destroy.

Small but Great

James 3:3–5

In verse 6 James takes his forest fire illustration to the next level by declaring that the tongue itself is a fire—a "world of unrighteousness," a destructive and immoral force powerful enough to wreak havoc on the same scale as a forest fire. The balance of verse 6 elaborates on the tongue's effects. It defiles and sets aflame. The last mention of "setting on fire" at the end of the verse describes the source of the tongue's fire as hell itself. This statement recharacterizes his description of the tongue from a generic flame to a more sinister weapon. We should not underestimate the potential destructive power of this small body part.

Small but Great: James draws upon tangible examples from our world to reinforce his point about the potentially destructive power of the tongue. In the same way that a horse's bit or a ship's rudder can direct the course of something far larger, the tongue can direct our entire body. And in the same way that a small flame can reduce an entire forest to ashes, the tongue can bring about massive destruction.

James supports his claims about the tongue with an example from nature, beginning in verse 7. A huge variety of creatures have been

Taming the Tongue: Every year people spend great sums to watch animals perform. Our ability to speak, among other things, allows us to train and direct animals, even ones far more powerful than we are. Amazing, right? But James uses this observation as a basis of comparison to highlight one thing few of us can tame: our tongue. This important part of our body exercises control over us, while it resists being controlled itself.

tamed by humans, ostensibly based on the power of the tongue. His observation here serves as the backdrop for a contrasting claim in verse 8. The human ability to speak is heralded as one of the distinctive traits that separate us from the animal kingdom. Speech also facilitates sophisticated communication among people and in our interaction with animals. Voice commands play a key role in taming and directing animals, a fact that James uses as a basis of contrast. It takes impressive skill to tame a lion or some other animal more powerful than we are. This is why people pay great sums to attend circuses or animal parks. What an incredible power we possess as humans! Is there anything we can't tame? "I'm glad you asked," James says, pointing to the tongue itself as an untamable force.

Human-controlled animal performances—from dolphin jumps to cattle herding and pet tricks—suggest we are pretty adept at getting things under control. But the tongue is a different animal altogether. James' description makes it sound as though no one can tame the tongue, especially since it is a restless evil and full of poison. Our only hope of controlling our tongues is God's power at work in us. Later in the book, James drills down on the source of our conflicts and quarrels (4:1), making clear that the tongue is simply an instrument by which we express and pursue the desires and pleasures that lie within us.

So what is the big problem with losing control of my speech? The comparisons to fire have already highlighted the destruction our tongue can cause to those around us. James now turns to the repercussions that an untamed tongue have for our relationship with God. What are the implications of blessing God out of one side of our mouths while cursing our fellow human beings—God's image-bearers—out of the other? James says this dual use of the tongue is symptomatic of a deeper problem: hypocrisy.

The Same Source?: So far James has treated our behavior in a binary fashion. For instance, we either have faith plus works or we don't; he hasn't really described a middle ground. This can create the impression that the life of faith James has in mind is achieved by a simple switch. But his discussion of the tongue illustrates the complexity of this new life. The totality of our behavior is what counts, not just the good things we do. If we bless God one minute and then curse those whom God has created, what does that tell us about the quality of our faith?

Blessing and cursing illustrate the same manner of problems that arise from claiming to have faith without any works to prove it. Even though we are fallen human beings, we are still made in the image of God. As our relationship with God is restored through faith in Jesus Christ, the sanctifying process of growth and maturity also restores our capacity as image-bearers. James' point here is that this change in our hearts should also be reflected in our behavior toward others, just as our works reflect our inner faith. But if we are cursing and denigrating those whom God has created, was does this say about our faith? Has there really been a change? James directs us away from such behavior by declaring that things ought not to be this way.

James offers some improbable scenarios to drive home the hypocrisy of continuing to curse others after we've supposedly begun to bless and worship God. In verse 11 he asks whether a spring can pour forth fresh and bitter water at the same time. The nature of liquid and osmosis make such an occurrence impossible. Without maintaining separation between the liquids, the fresh water becomes tainted and diluted by the bitter. The two cannot remain separate. The same logic holds true for believers in Christ. We cannot walk with God and sin at the same time. It is a one-or-the-other proposition.

The examples offered in verse 12 correlate source with output. My grandpa had an amazing knack for doing almost anything, including horticulture. He wanted to grow a variety of apples, but had limited space for an orchard. His solution? Grafting three different kinds of apples onto a single tree that grew a fourth variety. It was the coolest thing to see four different colors of apples growing from the same tree. But James reminds us that there are limitations to the changes we can bring about—things even my grandpa couldn't do. The roots of a fig tree are genetically predisposed to produce figs, so how can we expect the tree to produce olives? Can we expect figs to grow from a grapevine? The implied answer is, "No way!" Nor can a spring that is salty produce fresh water.

All of these examples reinforce the same point. Allowing sin in our lives—like showing partiality and dishonoring the poor—will impact the nature and quality of the spiritual fruit we bear. Something fundamental must change. And in the absence of such radical change, we are foolish to expect the outcome to be different. James is not recommending a minor change to our façade, but something much more substantial. If God has indeed changed our hearts, and we have matured through the trials he has allowed in our lives, then we should expect to see changes in the fruit our lives bear. If our lives don't produce the fruit that would match up with a life of faith, James challenges us to get to the root of the problem: our need for God's transformational power in our lives.

James 3:13–18

James introduces his next big idea using a rhetorical question phrased to expect a positive answer, as though there are some among his readers who are wise. This creates an interesting dynamic; it's as if he is asking all who think they are wise to raise their hands. James is not the one identifying the wise members of his audience—he leaves it up to individuals to identify themselves. Since being wise is a desirable and even enviable thing, this strategy virtually assures that the largest possible number of people will counts themselves the wise.

Wise and Understanding?: How can we know whether someone is truly wise? Is it their IQ or how much information they can bring to bear in any given situation? James offers an unexpected alternative that challenges our understanding of wisdom from a biblical standpoint. Just as faith without works is dead (2:26), so is "wisdom" that is not humbly put into practice.

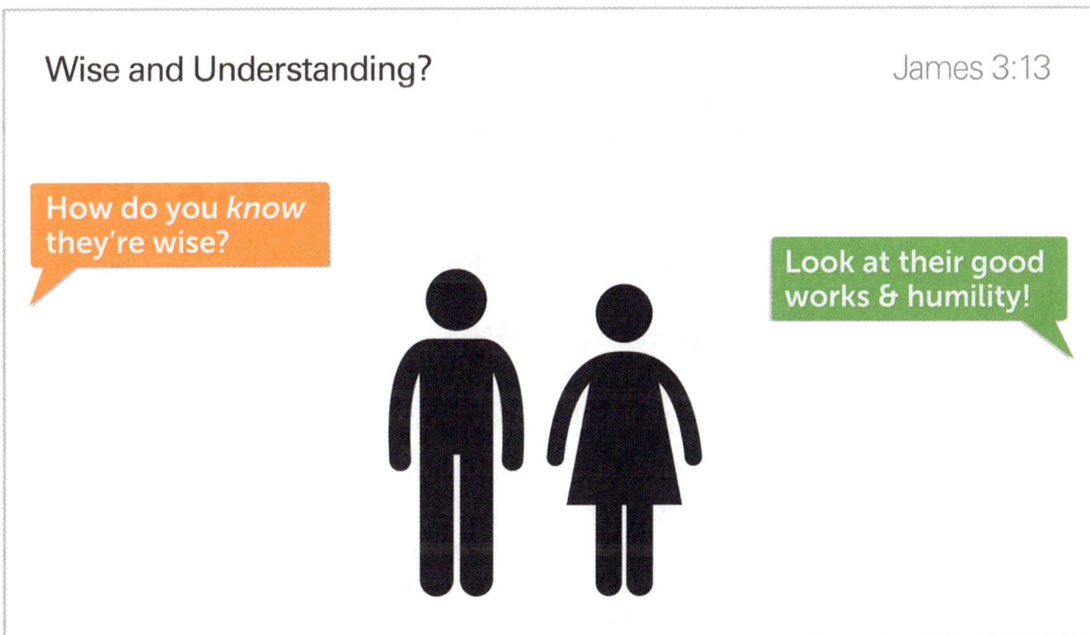

James could have introduced the same topic in several other ways, but none would have achieved as much buy-in. He could have simply said, "Those of you who consider yourselves to be wise and understanding, let them show it." But since this statement is less subjective, the people are less likely to self-nominate. The same would be true had James said, "If you are wise and understanding, then show it."

James' rhetorical question appeals to his readers' aspirational desire to be recognized for their wisdom and understanding. Who knows? Maybe he is going to call on them to shepherd and teach the unwise. Or perhaps he will bestow on them some special responsibility based on their enviable knowledge. Instead James takes things in an unexpected direction. In characteristic fashion, he reframes any notions about wisdom or understanding as a "put up or shut up" proposition. It takes more than a proclamation to attain this status. For James, wisdom must be demonstrated not only through a person's behavior, but by the humility they demonstrate in exercising their wisdom.

Why phrase things in this way? It would certainly have a chilling effect on anyone making false claims about having wisdom. How? By giving the believers around them a benchmark for distinguishing true, godly wisdom from a masquerade. James' pragmatic call to demonstrate wisdom through good behavior and humility effectively unmasks hypocrites whose actions cannot back up their claims. By inviting all who are wise and understanding to heed what he is about to say, James paves the ways for a stark shift in verse 14—away from where many of his audience may have expected him to go.

James shifts to bitter jealousy and selfish ambition seemingly out of nowhere. What do they have to do with wisdom? How can he jump from wisdom that demonstrates humility to talking about boasting and denying the truth? Has he shifted to a different topic? No, James is setting the stage for unmasking things that might look like wisdom but actually aren't.

James makes clear where this argument is heading in verse 15; he classifies the sinful behavior described in verse 14 as being a kind of wisdom—not a wisdom from above, but earthly, unspiritual, and even demonic wisdom. So how does all of this fit together?

Key Ingredients

James 3:14–17

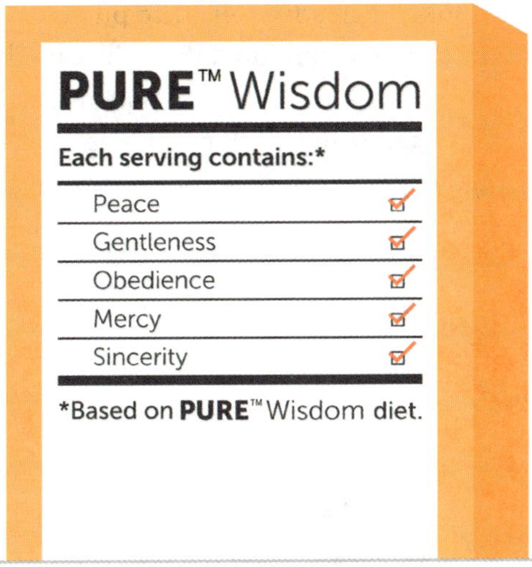

By calling on the wise to demonstrate their wisdom by humility and good behavior, James exposes those claiming to be wise even while their behavior is self-serving. The seeming contradiction of verses 13 and 14 is resolved in verse 15 by making clear that wise behavior is what counts, not just wise words. If actions are motivated by envy and ambition, if they lead to denials of the truth, then their so-called wisdom is revealed for what it is. It doesn't matter how eloquent their words or how grand their insights are. Their behavior betrays the origins of their knowledge.

Who in the world would consider such behavior a sign of wisdom, we might ask? I doubt that those who are peddling it say, "Step right up and I'll show you how my wisdom can advance your envious and jealous goals!" That's not how things work, not then and not now. You see, almost any biblical idea, when taken out of context or to an extreme, can be contorted for self-serving gain. And that gain needn't be only monetary; honor, attention, or prestige can be just as enticing a motive.

By beginning with the positive perspective of what godly wisdom looks like in practice, James provides a contrasting illustration so

Key Ingredients: We might think of wisdom primarily as knowledge, but James challenges this notion by describing qualities we can expect to see in someone who is truly wise. He contrasts this portrait of "wisdom from above" with one that is unspiritual, earthly, and even demonic. This earthly variety correlates jealousy and selfish ambition. In contrast, wisdom from above—what James classifies as true wisdom—is characterized by peace, gentleness, obedience, mercy, and sincerity.

Earthly and Evil: Instead of viewing wisdom as a certain type of knowledge, James contrasts two different sources of wisdom based on the results they bring about. In other words, it's what inside that counts, not the fancy packaging. Figuratively speaking, wisdom from above can be clearly differentiated from earthly wisdom by looking at what pours forth from it.

readers can more objectively evaluate those claiming to be wise. He then applies these contrasting portraits to the interpersonal relationships of his audience in verses 16–17. Instead of knowing a tree by its fruit (Matt 7:15–20), James' analogy is more like "where there's smoke, there's fire." If these purveyors of wisdom are characterized by envy and ambition, they will leave disorder and evil in their wake. This is the demonic wisdom mentioned in verse 16, standing in stark contrast to the wisdom coming from above described in verse 17. If the wisdom is pure, peaceful, gentle, obedient, full of mercy and good fruit, then its heavenly origins are obvious.

Earthly and Evil

James 3:15–16

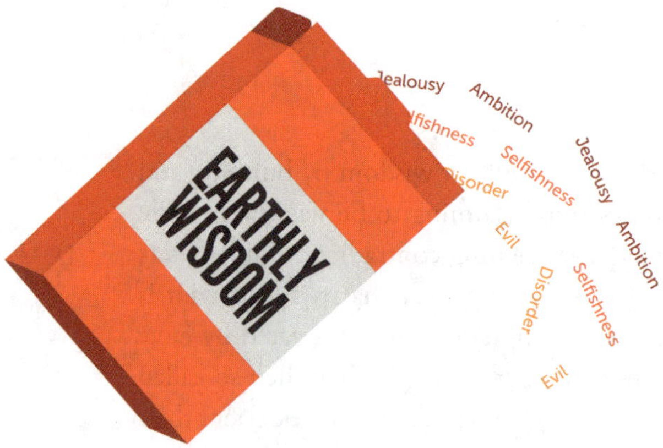

These contrasting pictures of wisdom serve as a litmus test for evaluating the worth of someone's claim to wisdom. How does that wisdom impact their life and the lives of those around them? Does it lead to peace and humility or to infighting and broken relationships? These tests allow us to strip away any fancy veneer people use to obscure the origins and motivation of their wisdom. They serve as a safeguard for us. Examining the contrasts may not change people's view of themselves, but it can protect us from being misled by a slick-sounding presentation.

For those who truly want to be considered wise, James raises the bar on what it takes to achieve this goal. Wisdom requires much more than head knowledge and intelligent argumentation. It takes God working in and through us to impact those around us. The big take-away here is that the fruit of wisdom from above offers more compelling evidence of its existence than a well-reasoned argument. Those who pursue heavenly wisdom are rewarded with peace (verse 18), and as peacemakers, they are able to reap a harvest of righteousness. Two sources of wisdom; two very different outcomes. Which will you choose?

James 4

James 4:1–12

James introduces his next big idea using another rhetorical question, this time about the source of conflicts and quarrels. Rhetorical questions do more than just announce the topic; they challenge us to think about answers *we* might give before James provides his own. If our answers differ from his, then we are more inclined to listen to his teachings about the matter. Even if we arrive at the same answer, we are motivated to compare how the other person arrived at their conclusion and learn from them. The bottom line is that rhetorical questions can bring about a much deeper level of engagement with an audience, compared with simply announcing, "Now we will discuss ________."

The Power of Rhetorical Questions

Rhetorical questions aren't just an ancient Greek convention. They still serve as a powerful tool to foster deeper engagement. If you are teaching a group, you could use the same strategy in your own introduction by asking a question and offering some potential answers. Ask those in the group what they might answer and why. All of this can set the stage for a rich conversation of the passage.

What kinds of answers might come to mind about the source of conflicts and quarrels? My first inclination is to focus on the role that others play: "If it hadn't been for ______, then none of this conflict would have happened." If I can blame things on someone else, then there is less of a need for me to consider my own responsibility in a conflict. Others might blame it on the devil for tempting them or name "sin" as the generic answer for all of the world's woes. The main point here is to recognize the lengths to which James has gone to engage his readers in the teaching that follows. Calling us to answer a rhetorical question creates a great teachable moment.

Ultimate Source of Conflict

James 4:1–3

Ultimate Source of Conflict: James poses a rhetorical question about the source of conflict in our lives. How would you respond? What sources come to mind? We might first think of external causes that allow us to avoid taking responsibility. But James directs us to look inside, to the role played by our desires, envy, and motives.

James' answer to his question is rhetorically loaded. Why? He answers with another question, one that anticipates agreement and acceptance from the reader. But instead of just saying conflicts and quarrels stem from our pleasures, James uses another device to draw attention to the answer. The word "this" in the ESV, NET, and LEB of verse 1 is a forward-pointing reference: "Is it not from *this*: from your pleasures …" (LEB). Other translations omit the extra reference. The value of forward-pointing references is their ability to delay the introduction of a target idea, thus drawing special attention to it. Regardless of how 4:1 is translated, the original verse's two rhetorical questions, coupled with the forward-pointing reference and target, highlight the importance James places on the role of our desires and pleasures.

Instead of simply condemning pleasures and desires as evil, James focuses on the damage they can cause when allowed to flourish unchecked by moral restraint. The problem is not the desire itself, but the dwelling or acting on it that can result. We all face temptations every day; this is just part of life in a fallen world awaiting final restoration (see Rom 8:18–23). Paul describes the unsaved person as a slave to sin, but believers have been set free from this slavery to serve God (Rom 6:6–7; 7:5–6). So as we face these temptations, the million-dollar question is how we will respond to this new freedom. Will we choose to set our mind on these desires, or on following God's Spirit (Rom 8:5–6)? Until the Lord returns and we receive glorified bodies, we will face an ongoing battle with our fleshly desires. Although we have been set free from slavery to sin, we now have a choice about whom we will serve: "For just as you presented your members as slaves to immorality and lawlessness, leading to lawlessness, so now present your members as slaves to righteousness, leading to sanctification" (Rom 6:19).

Ultimate Source — James 4:1–3

The warfare language James uses in chapter 4 parallels Paul's portrayal of our ongoing battle between serving God and serving our fleshly desires. James casts the desires in a negative light. They aren't healthy desires that edify and build us up—they bring us to battle with what we know is right or lead us to wage war against others. James implies that these desires compel us to serve our flesh instead of God.

James offers a few examples in the first half of verse 2. The desire to have something we lack can be powerful enough to lead us to murder. James may well be using hyperbole here, but it creates a powerful image for us to ponder. His next example is a bit less

Ultimate Source: It can be tempting to blame our conflicts solely on others without considering the role our passions and desires play. James points out that our conflicts with others or with God have their origins inside of us—the war that our desires and passions are waging against each other spills out in our interactions with others.

extreme but still harmful: The unmet or unfulfilled desire leads to fighting and quarreling.

In the second half of verse 2, James shifts from describing the behavior to diagnosing the root problem in the "because" statements at the end of verse 2 and in verse 3. Although people desire something, they don't receive it because they have not asked for it. The implication here is that they have not asked the Lord for the desired thing in prayer. For those who have asked (verse 3), they haven't received it because they have asked with wrong motives. They don't desire the lacking thing for edification or building up, but to consume for their own selfish pleasure. This implies that we cannot expect the Lord to give us what we do not truly need. There are limitations on what we can expect the Lord to provide for us, and James says the motivation and intent behind our requests play a big role in determining the outcome.

James signals a transition in verse 4 with a little name-calling. The last time James directly addressed his readers, he referred to them as "my brothers" (see 3:1, 10, 12), fostering a warm sense of family. Now he calls them "adulterers" or "adulterous people"! It is clear from the context that he is not addressing some new group of people. The change in expression indicates how James' view of his audience changes in light of the topic he is tackling, and his view of them also affects how they view themselves. In his view, people who give themselves over to unbridled pursuit of their desires are appropriately classified as adulterers. They have forsaken their commitment to God, just like a wayward spouse. James likens the selfish pursuit of our desires, whatever they may be, to the unashamed indulgence of desire that leads to extramarital sin.

James couples this change of reference with another attention-getting device: the rhetorical question, "Don't you know…?" Instead of equating friendship with the world with being an enemy of God, James asks a question that implies his readers should already know this to be true. In the second half of verse 4, "therefore" formally introduces the conclusion we should draw from the preceding discussion. James also rephrases the idea in terms of desired outcome instead of objective fact: "Whoever wants to be a friend of the world…." This shift highlights the role that our choice plays in the matter. We are not helpless victims; our response to our desires directly affects our relationship with God.

Frenemies?

James 4:4

Would a follower of Jesus would wake up one morning and decide to befriend the world in order to be an enemy of God? Not likely. More likely this friendship would grow slowly over time, maybe even in the name of being "all things to all people" (1 Cor 9:22). After all, who would intentionally make themselves God's enemy? This is precisely the point James is making here. He wants us to clearly understand the implications and consequences of our decisions. Although we may believe that indulging our desires is innocuous, doing so can have dire spiritual consequences. Understanding this can deter us from giving in to sinful desires and help us consider the outcome of our decisions.

Frenemies?: Is it possible to be friends and enemies at the same time? Not in our relationship with God. We cannot devote ourselves to God and the world at the same time. If we choose to make friends with the world, we also choose to make an enemy of God. We cannot serve two masters (Matt 6:24). Being a frenemy of God is not an option.

In verses 5–6, James turns to the Old Testament to bolster his claims. Verse 5 asserts that God has placed a spirit within us, one that he jealously desires to be focused on him. There is some debate about which spirit James means here—ours, or the Holy Spirit. His mention about "giving greater grace" in verse 6 points toward it meaning our spirit, but the matter is certainly open to debate. The main takeaway is that God supplies his grace to ensure that the indwelling spirit—our regenerated spirit or God's holy one—would indeed turn toward him instead of turning away toward other objects of affection.

James bolsters his claim about God's grace in verse 6 with a quote from Proverbs 3:34. This proverb offers a corollary to verse 5 by looking at both sides of the issue instead of one. Although the proverb affirms the statement in verse 5 that God is a giver of grace, Proverbs is more specific about who receives that grace. It describes contrasting groups: the proud and the humble. From this perspective, only the humble receive grace. And what about the proud, what can they expect to receive? Instead of God's grace and support, they are told to expect his opposition. James leaves the exact nature of the opposition unstated, but one thing is clear. His imagery reinforces the claim in verse 4 that pursuing our desires instead of God makes us his enemy.

So far in chapter 4 James has focused on the root causes of conflicts and quarrels and the negative consequences they have on our relationship with God. In verse 7 he transitions to the positive steps we can take to prevent conflicts in the first place. How can knowing their source help prevent them? What steps can we take to avoid becoming an enemy of God?

James presents the answers in a staccato list of exhortations in verses 7–10. His first command is to submit ourselves to God. What does this look like? Based on the preceding verses, it would entail submitting our desires and pursuit of pleasures to God. What's next? Resisting the devil, which comes with something of a promise. James' phrasing here implies a natural reaction to our resistance: If we resist, the devil will flee from us. This offers us great encouragement as we face spiritual battles. Instead of fearing the devil's power, we can take confidence in the outcome of our submission to God.

James describes another action/reaction pair beginning in verse 8. It, too, offers an implicit promise that as we draw near to God, he in turn will draw near to us. We can find great encouragement in this promise during those times we feel distant from him, either as a result of sinful choices we've made or of other factors. We can have great confidence as we draw near to him that he will reciprocate.

One of the great hurdles for us to overcome is to truly believe this is possible. Our human inclination is to promote ourselves—to look out for our own interests even at the expense of others. It makes no sense to believe that humbling ourselves has a payoff, right? But this clash with conventional wisdom underlines the magnitude of the spiritual problem—obeying God's commands contradicts common sense. So it boils down to whether we are going to trust God and offer him our allegiance, or align ourselves with the world.

Initiative + Response: In contrast to the negative relationship James describes in 4:1–6, here he introduces a positive cause/effect relationship. Pursuing our pleasures rather than God is the root of conflict and quarrels. But as we choose to humble ourselves and draw near to God, we can expect him to draw near to us—and the devil to flee. Our choices determine the outcome; which path will you choose?

James phrases the next two commands in verse 8 as if he is addressing different groups—the sinners and the double-minded. Based on the nature of his preceding exhortations, these shifts have the same rhetorical effect as his reference to adulterers in verse 4. His calls to be humble and draw near to God clash with the terms he uses to address the audience in his next exhortation. In calling sinners, not just believers, to cleanse or wash their hands, James implies that they should not just clean their hands once; they should stop sinning so they don't become soiled in the first place. The same holds true when he calls the double-minded to purify their hearts. It is akin to saying that if their hearts had been purified in the first place, they would not have been double-minded. James resorts to name-calling here to create thematic amplification for each exhortation. Doing so packs more punch into a tiny package than the simple exhortation to stop sinning or to purify one's hands.

James continues his litany of exhortations in verse 9, building on the preceding ones. The calls to lament, mourn, and weep are associated with hearing horrible news. If there were a tragic death or some natural disaster, these actions would be appropriate expressions of grief. But James is addressing a believer's response to conflict and quarrels. For him, the tragedy is that this kind of behavior is found among believers—much as Paul said in 1 Corinthians 6:6. More tragic still is the need to direct them to consider that their unbridled passions are the root cause. James invokes the language of mourning and lament to emphasize the severity of the situation.

We would do well to take these matters as seriously as James does rather than viewing his remarks as rhetorical overstatement. In my own life, I know I would much rather not see myself as the one responsible for a broken or fractured relationship. Blaming it on someone else is much easier than honestly considering my own role in the debacle. Metaphors of mourning and lament move far beyond saying "I'm sorry"—they are external manifestations of an inner attitude. "I'm sorry" can mean simply I'm sorry I got caught, not necessarily that I feel any genuine remorse for the hurt I have caused. Lament requires accepting responsibility for the fallout of my behavior and commitment to change to prevent future harm.

Weeping and lament hold significance for another reason that we often overlook in our modern, individualistic culture: They allow others to actually witness our decision to change. Although some might make a show merely for the attention, public lament has a way of putting you on the hook to follow through on your vow to change. The same holds true for confessing our sins to one another, something James advocates in 5:16. If others are aware of the commitment I've made, it's much more difficult to change my mind—at least this is how it *ought* to work, though it seems people are becoming more willing to give me a pass. It's as if we all have an agreement: "I'll let you slide on this one if you do the same for me." It's an uncommon relationship in which people truly hold each other accountable.

James highlights one of the keys to true repentance in verse 10: humility. Not only does he call us to humble ourselves before the Lord, he says that the Lord will exalt us for doing so. Think about that for a minute. James began this section focusing on the cause of conflicts and quarrels—giving way to our pleasures and desires. We could also reframe this problem in terms of selfishness versus humility. Most conflicts involve one person placing a higher value on their own interests to the detriment of the other person's. Paul redirects us from this sinful tendency in Philippians 2:3–4, saying, "*Do* nothing according to selfish ambition or according to empty conceit, but in humility considering one another better than yourselves, each of you not looking out for your own interests, but also each of you *for* the interests of others." A natural consequence of putting other's needs before our own is keeping our own desires in check. Taking such a path all but guarantees we will avoid conflict and quarrels. And humbling ourselves in this way comes with the bonus of God exalting us when it is appropriate (1 Pet 5:6). What a contrast to *us* exalting ourselves and letting our pleasures rule.

In verses 11–12, James tackles another issue related to conflict: speaking evil against one another. Instead of appealing to our compassion for the other person, or to our conscience, James chooses fear as the motivator. He explains that we are not just maligning another believer; we are maligning God's law. Remember how the addressees of this letter were described in 1:1? Jewish believers, the twelve tribes of Israel scattered by persecution. The pressure of persecution can lead some to turn on others to save themselves, forsaking the larger community of faith. In James' view, when we speak evil or judge other believers, the consequences are far graver than we might have expected. But wait—it gets worse. Instead of being a doer of the law—as he advocates in 1:22–25—we make ourselves *judges* of the law. Why is that a big deal? Well, criticizing the law also entails criticizing the one who gave it: God. Not only is he the lawgiver, but judgment is *his* prerogative, not ours. In verse 12, James includes the chilling reminder that God is the one who is able to save or destroy.

Speaking Evil: When we speak badly of other believers, James tells us that we are actually doing far more: We are maligning God's law and the giver of that law too! Speaking to others in this way is equivalent to judging them, and judgment is reserved for God alone. So as we consider how to respond when we're frustrated or angry with others, James challenges us to carefully consider the consequences of our behavior. If we shake our fist at others, we are also shaking it at God's law and him as judge. Is venting our anger really worth that?

Looking at the issue in this way completely changes what we might describe as venting at or losing our temper with other believers. James removes any wiggle room for us to justify or condone our behavior. While we might be willing to lose control of our words with another believer, would we really do that with God? No way! Especially bearing in mind: He is the one who saves or destroys. James closes the section by asking a question that he leaves unanswered: Who are we to behave this way? His implication is that, by taking the role of judge for ourselves, we are acting as if we are God's equals.

James 4:13–17

In the final section of chapter 4, James addresses the problem of boasting about the future. He puts words in the mouth of a hypothetical person who presumes to go to such-and-such a place for a year to do business and make a quick buck. So what is the big idea for this section? "Don't be presumptuous, but instead preface your statements with 'If the Lord wills…' to demonstrate that you are holding you plans in an open hand," or something along those lines.

James tells us that we are a vapor, here today and gone tomorrow. This means we shouldn't make hard and fast plans because they might all come to naught, right? But this notion leaves several issues unreconciled. First, what does this have to do with the preceding section about governing your passions instead of letting them run wild? Nothing really. What about where James ends this section with his application in verse 17? How does making presumptuous plans relate to not doing the good you know you ought to do? My goal in this commentary is to better understand the flow of the writer's argument. We need to make sure we don't get off track from where I think James has been heading all along.

The preceding section (verses 1–12) deals with problems arising from not governing our passions and desires. James uses the icebreaker question, "Where do conflicts and quarrels come from?," to get us thinking of potential causes. The particular cause he focuses on is our selfish desire to have our wants and passions fulfilled. This, James says, is the real root of our interpersonal conflicts (verse 2). After diagnosing the source of our problems in verses 1–6, James describes steps we can take to ensure that our passions don't run roughshod over other people (verses 7–10). He closes the section exhorting us not to speak evil of others, potentially an example of how unbridled passions can lead us to usurp God's place as judge.

Vaporizing Plans: James begins the section introducing hypothetical people who decide to go off to such-and-such a place to trade and earn a profit. What could be wrong with that? Maybe not what you think. Reconciling these verses with those at the end of the section require us to dig a bit deeper than the sin of presumption.

So is there a connection between this section and the last? Is it a brand new topic or a continuation of James' teaching about keeping our passions and desires in line with God's? There are no formal markers in the grammar to indicate that verse 13–17 must be taken as a new section. There is a transition, but one that is best understood as another example of an area where our desires and passions can end up supplanting God's plans and desires for us. In it, James highlights an area in which our selfishness can make us deaf and blind to doing the very things that God redeemed us for in the first place.

The pursuit of our passions can overtake our pursuit of doing the "good works, which God prepared beforehand, so that we may walk in them" (Eph 2:10). Now let's slow down and read through the text more carefully so that we don't miss the connections that tie this chapter together.

James begins in verse 13 by introducing a potential subgroup of his audience: those who boast about future plans. But verse 13 serves only to introduce the group he is addressing. "Come now" is the ancient Greek version of a coach getting her team's attention by saying, "Listen up!" James wants them to listen because what he's about to say will come like a slap in the face. These people are the very ones who don't know about tomorrow, who don't really understand what a life is like. Not the affirmation entrepreneurial believers are looking for, is it? What is their life like? A smoky vapor, one that appears for a short time and before it's gone.

So is James condemning presumptuous planning here, or is he focused on something more? We'll find the answers in verses 15–17, but we must make sure we are not reading something into them that isn't there. In contrast with the speech of the merchants in verse 13, James offers a positive reformulation of the qualities that should characterize our speech. His positive version includes a condition that must be met before the rest of it is possible: If the Lord wills. We can think of this as asking the Lord's permission: "May we do X?" Here the focus is only on doing X, asking a yes or no question. But I do not believe permission is what James has in mind.

Another way of understanding this condition is as a comparison of this option over against other alternatives, say, between X and Y. In other words, is *this* what the Lord would have me do, or should I be doing something else instead? In this view, the condition is focused on direction—determining what God would have us do, so as not to get distracted by the wrong things. What might distract us from the good things we ought to be doing? How about our selfish desires and pleasures? They lead us to arrogantly boast about our capabilities: "Oh yeah, well I can ______!" Fill in the blank. James tells us in verse 16 that whatever it is that drives us to talk about our big plans stems from arrogance, and it is evil.

I do not believe that James is talking only about making presumptuous plans. He isn't encouraging us to tack on "If the Lord wills…" to hedge our bets since, who knows, we might just get hit by a bus before we can go and do whatever it is we were boasting about. No! Instead, James is concerned with making plans for the future without ever considering—or asking—what God already has planned for us.

Vaporizing Plans: In this verse, rather than focusing on whether we have God's permission to do X, James calls us to a higher standard. Instead of presumptuously asking *permission*, we should ask *direction*. What would God have us pursue?

The book of James gets a bad rap for teaching things that seem to contradict the teaching we find in Paul's letters. But James and Paul are on precisely the same page here at the end of chapter 4. Both believe that God has created us for good works and that he fully intends for us to do them (see Eph 2:10). In fact, James goes one step beyond Paul by claiming that if we choose to do something other than the good God has willed for us to do, then we are sinning against him. The desire to pursue our own pleasures and follow our boastful desires has the power to trump God's good and perfect will for us and distract us from his plan.

God is not a cosmic parent from whom we must ask permission before we can do anything. He is the Creator of the universe. He created us with such intentionality that he even planned out the good things he would have us do as part of his bigger plan. This is an important reason why he redeemed us from our fallen state: so that we could get back to doing what it was he created us for in the first place! What does God think about us going off track and doing our own thing in place of the good that he intended? He views it as arrogant and boastful. Think about it: Who are we to know better than God what we ought to be doing? Am I really smarter than God?

No way! But this is precisely what I am communicating to him when I ignore what he has for me and make my own choices instead.

Does this mean that I should live in fear of accidently stepping off the path of God's perfect will for me, as though it is some kind of divine balance beam? James doesn't go into that much detail, nor does Paul in Ephesians 2:10. But both are clear that God has plans for us. Instead of just going off and doing our own thing to the exclusion of God's plan, we need to make sure we are looking to him for guidance. And from James' perspective, one of the greatest obstacles we face in doing the good God plans for us is allowing our desires and pleasures to run our lives. Making the choice to become friends with the world and pursue our own wants means making ourselves God's enemies. But if we direct our desires toward God instead, just as he intended (Jas 4:5), we can expect a different outcome. We can experience a greater grace through an ever-narrowing gap as we humble ourselves and draw closer to him.

James 5

James 5:1–6

James signals the transition to his next main section using several devices. The first is his call to "come now," which is ancient Greek for "You! Listen up!" It is a call to pay attention just as in 4:13, when he calls a specific group of people to listen closely. Who is it this time? "You rich people." *Which* rich people? Well, scholars are divided on this issue. Some believe James is addressing the rich believers in his audience, while others believe he is prophetically addressing unbelievers who may never hear his words. We have no way of knowing which is correct; arguments can be made in both directions. But this ambiguity may be intentional on James' part.

By first telling his audience "y'all come" and then narrowing down to "you rich ones," James does something important. He makes it much harder for us to exclude ourselves from this group with material wealth. Compare this to if he had addressed "those rich people" as if none was present in the audience. Or if he had said, "You rich ones, weep...." See the difference? James' comments certainly apply beyond the bounds of his immediate hearers. But by phrasing his statement to directly address his immediate audience, James puts the fear of God into anyone of means who hears his exhortations. As modern readers, we too have become part of this audience he addresses.

Now let's contrast how James portrays wealth with how we tend to think about it. We prize wealth, storing it in vaults to keep it safe. No one wants to lose money. In fact, we cling to it so much that we have special words like "philanthropy" to describe giving money away to those who haven't earned it in some way. Even in our credit- and cash-driven society, silver and gold are still highly prized. Investing in precious metals is touted as a safeguard against inflation or a failed currency, right? Now let's look at James' description of wealth.

In verse 1 he tells the rich to weep and cry over what lies ahead, creating a parallel with the kind of mourning over pride and sin he described in 4:8–10. In English we would much more naturally use rhetorical questions to link the statements, but in Greek the description of the miseries is broken into two parts: a statement and support for it. The first bit introduces the idea of miseries; the second discloses that they are coming down the pike. This second bit of info answers the question, "Which ones?" In this case, no miseries have been mentioned. The extra information recharacterizes the miseries—an ominous and unexpected warning.

What's Coming?: James uses a series of paired statements to point out the coming miseries that the rich will face. In English, these statements would be most naturally linked by rhetorical questions, whereas Greek uses a conjunction generally translated "for." By unpacking things one bit at a time, James discloses that the present comfort the rich experience will not last forever.

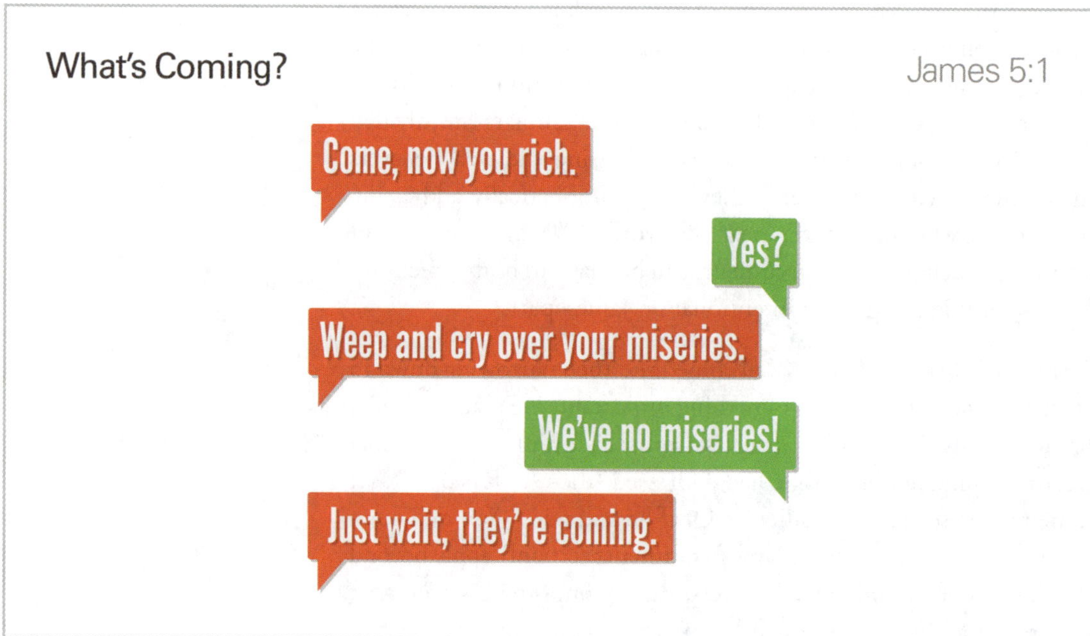

What miseries lie ahead? Seeing all of their wealth—the things in which the rich have placed their hope—become worthless. Back in the ancient times, gold and silver weren't the only forms of currency. Clothing was also used as payment for bartering or stored as a form of savings. This is why Naaman offers clothing, along with his silver, to Elisha and Gehazi as payment for healing him along in 2 Kings 5:20–24. It wasn't because the two were poorly dressed, but because clothes were a valuable commodity, just like silver. The ancients would also store up crops and other commodities as a source of revenue, just as pictured in the parable of the Rich Fool (Luke 12:16–21). This is why James describes wealth as rotting and clothing as becoming moth-eaten. People weren't concerned about an economic recession ruining their investments; natural causes were enough to destroy their holdings.

So what image is James after here? A modern equivalent might be identity theft. Imagine going to make a large purchase after investing lots of time and energy into saving up the needed funds. Then imagine learning that your check bounced because there are no funds in your account. "What? No funds? Where did they go?" It is very easy to place our confidence in our resources instead of in God, but wealth disappears.

Think of it like this: Our whole life is one giant investment opportunity. We constantly face choices about how we'll choose to invest our lives. Will it be in our job? Our awards and recognition? Our dream vacations? Our 401(k) accounts? James challenges us to consider how our investments will pay off in God's eyes. What return will these investments have on our relationship with him? James' answer is pretty shocking. In the end, investing in earthly riches is a waste. Why? They don't last—and they don't have eternal value.

This is precisely the point Jesus makes in Matthew 6:19–21: "Do not store up for yourselves treasures on earth, where moth and consuming insect destroy and where thieves break in and steal, but store up for yourselves treasures in heaven, where neither moth nor consuming insect destroy and where thieves do not break in or steal. For where your treasure is, there your heart will be also." Jesus points out the destructive forces that can rob you of your savings; James points out the response that results from that destruction: weeping and mourning.

Now if we circle back to James' opening call in verse 1, to cry and weep aloud, we are in a better position to understand the point he is making. You don't have to be rich to squander your life. Anyone can choose to invest their time and energy in things that have no eternal value from God's perspective. Hearing this proclamation addressed to the rich—whomever James may have meant—should give us pause to sit back and consider our personal investment strategy.

Lasting Investment

James 5:2–3

Lasting Investment: What things are we confidently storing up and placing our trust in? Are they eternal things? James reminds us that earthly riches will not last. In ancient times, natural causes like pests and corrosion threatened to destroy someone's saving. Now, we face threats of identity theft, recession, and inflation. James presents a timeless challenge: to consider the dividends our investments pay. Are we investing in spiritual things that will last, or in material things that are ephemeral?

Throughout this book, James has offered a sobering look at the detrimental influence money can have. We would expect him to warn the rich about boasting in their wealth, but in 1:10–11 he says they should boast in their humiliation based on the perishable nature of wealth. Then in 2:1–7, he highlights the deferential treatment the rich receive compared to the poor, pointing out that the rich are the ones mistreating his listeners, not the poor. Why should the poor be dishonored and the rich abusers honored by deferential treatment? Why make any distinction in the first place? In James 4:2, he points out that lack of riches can lead to envy, and thus to quarrels and fights. Finally in 4:11–16, James offers an illustration that reveals how focusing on fulfilling our own desires can distract us from doing the good that God has called us to do. In none of these cases does James condemn riches as evil. Instead, he teaches in keeping with Paul's assertion that "the love of money is a root of all kinds of evils" (1 Tim 6:10 ESV). Money itself isn't amoral, but its ability to corrupt cannot be overstated.

So if wealth is not inherently evil, then what problem is James is getting at? We find the key in the descriptions in verses 2–3. The problem is not *having* wealth, but what we are *doing* with it—

or more precisely, what we are *not* doing with it. James portrays the rich sitting on their wealth instead of using it to accomplish something meaningful. Just as the rich fool dies before he can enjoy his wealth, James warns the rich their savings will be destroyed before they are able to spend them. The *storage* of wealth is what leads to its destruction by pests and corrosion, and this corrosion is what will testify against them (verse 3). If the rich had used their wealth for good instead of hoarding it, then the moths, rot, and corrosion would not have destroyed it.

James then offers a chilling warning at end of verse 3. All the wealth the rich have hoarded will not result in anything of eternal value. Instead of storing up something that leads to praise—"Well done, good and faithful servant" (Matt 25:21–23 ESV)—James depicts investments as toxic, a poison that will consume its owner's flesh like fire. The holdings they valued so greatly will be Exhibit A in the case against them in the final judgment.

James has already said that the problem is not in having wealth, but doing something with it—stewarding instead of hoarding. In verse 4, he offers an example of the effect of hoarding. In this case, James describes wealth as money that is owed but withheld from workers. In contrast to the good stewardship of the first two servants in the parable of the Talents (see Matt 25:14–30), the greed of the rich leads them to cling to their riches instead of properly stewarding their use. Here, the unpaid workers become Exhibit B in the case against the hoarders. James uses the same kind of two-part format to introduce the workers as did to introduce the coming miseries in verse 1. The wages he refers to in verse 4 first belong to the workers reaping in the fields of the rich. The second part further characterizes the wages as what the rich hold back instead of paying.

Why would the rich withhold the wages for work that's been done? We find the answer in verse 5. Instead of paying what is owed, the wealthy divert the money to self-indulgence and luxury. This recasts them as not as rich as we thought. If they really had such an excess, they would be able to pay their obligations and have money left to live on. James portrays the rich as more interested in continuing their overextended lifestyle than in honoring God (and their workers) with the wealth due him (and them).

Payment Due

James 5:4–6

Payment Due: James paints a picture of the rich having extra in part because they withhold the wages due to their workers. Although the wealth may offer them momentary comfort and security, a day of reckoning is coming. When it arrives, both the unpaid workers and the withheld wages will bear witness against them.

They forsake their obligations so they can continue indulging their selfish desires. The second part of verse 5 likens them to the proverbial fatted calf. All of the excess they enjoyed actually fattened them for the day of slaughter.

This ancient picture of indulgence has a modern equivalent: living beyond one's means on credit while not paying one's creditors. I know there are predatory lenders and naïve borrowers, but the appeal of credit is the opportunity to enjoy now and defer the consequences until later. Both situations arise from overindulgence and persist because of an unwillingness to humble oneself.

Verse 6 broadens the discussion from owner/worker relationships to look more generally at the relationship between rich and poor. James portrays the disadvantaged as righteous, condemned and murdered by the rich. This is the same image of the rich he invokes in 2:6 by asserting that the rich are the ones dragging the poor to court. In chapter 2, the poor are dishonored and mistreated, but there is no mention of their response. Likewise in 5:6, the poor offer no resistance to the schemes of the rich. It's like they have just given up.

So where does this looming judgment of the rich leave those who are helplessly suffering at their hands? James takes this up in verse 7, but we should not overlook the function of his warning to the rich. History offers many examples of attempts to address the inequity between rich and poor—from riots and revolution to resigned acceptance. How should believers respond? James' answer becomes the big idea for the next section.

James 5:7–12

Most every English version of the Bible begins a new section at verse 7. Although there are good reasons for making a break here, it can make it seem as though what follows is somehow unrelated to what precedes. The word in verse 7 translated "therefore" in most versions signals a transition from singling out the rich in 5:1 to addressing the broader audience about the issues raised. How should believers respond to situations over which they have no control? With patience. Patience for what? The assurance that the Lord himself will take care of such matters upon his return. In fact, James uses a Greek emphatic expression to highlight the importance of "coming of the Lord." This reminder serves a dual purpose: To those who feel powerless to counter the advantage that riches can offer, James offers the assurance that the rich will be judged, whether it be in this life or in the next. The second purpose of the reminder is more subtle.

What serves as hopeful assurance to the oppressed also serves as ominous warning to the oppressor. This fast-forward glimpse of the final judgment shatters any confidence the rich might have that their behavior has gone unnoticed. On the contrary, their hoarded riches—along with the cries of those whom they oppressed—bear testimony against them. They should not mistake God's present inaction for indifference. There will indeed be a day of reckoning. The open question is this: What will each of us do to prepare for it? In 4:17, James offered an admonition to the presumptuous that applies equally well here: "Therefore, to the one who knows to do good and does not do it, to him it is sin." If you owe your workers their wages, then pay them. If there are needs to be met, and we have the means to meet them, then we must do it. But choosing not to do the good that it is within our power will be counted against us as sin in that final day. The folly of hoarding and self-indulgence will be revealed and dealt with.

And the Answer Is... James 5:7,9,12

And the Answer Is...: In these verses, James offers a series of exhortations based on a single motivation: coming judgment. In verses 8 and 9, he bolsters each exhortation with the reminder that we will give an account for our behavior. The Lord's return serves both as an encouragement to obey and a deterrent from continuing sinful behavior.

James doesn't leave us to take his word for it. He offers a practical example to support his call for patience. The experience of the farmer offers proof that patience pays off in the end. He introduces the example using the attention-getter "behold." The farmer's crops are "the precious fruit of the soil," not just the expected outcome of planting. At the end of verse 7, James elaborated on his initial statement about the farmer waiting; he uses the same verb for being patient that he used in the command at the beginning of the verse. He refers to the early and late rains to point to the necessary passage of time for the crops to mature—hence the need for patience. James ties back to his initial command in verse 7 by reiterating it in verse 8. He strengthens the link between the illustration and the original command by using "also/too." Just as the farmer is patient, *we also* must be patient. Note that James' call for patience has a similar outcome but a different focus than Paul's appeal to leave vengeance to the Lord in Romans 12:19. Whereas Paul appeals to his audience not to usurp a divine role, James relies on the surety and proximity of the Lord's judgment. James emphasizes the role of patience, whereas Paul highlights our need to refrain from taking vengeance. James explicitly grounds his call for strengthened hearts in nearness of the Lord's coming (verse 8b). This reminder of his imminent return is as if to say, "It's not much longer, so hang in there!"

To-Do List: How should we respond to the injustice of the rich oppressing the poor? While it is human nature to react in anger and hostility, James exhorts believers to be patient and to leave everything in God's hands. After all, his return is near.

In verse 9 James moves on to other situations around us with which we might disagree. But instead of offering a specific context, such as the rich withholding wages, he calls us not to complain against one another. Why not? Once again he bases this exhortation on what it would lead to—namely judgment. In the second half of the verse, James uses the same attention-getter, "behold," as in verse 7. But instead of introducing an example he introduces the Judge, emphasizing the nearness of his coming.

This appeal to the Lord's imminent return reminds me of how I would react to the "imminent return" of my parents when I was growing up. When they left to do errands, they would often give me chores that they expected to be done by the time they returned. I was prone to procrastinate, telling myself I would play or read just a little while longer. Everything would suddenly change when I realized what time it was, or worse—when I heard the garage door opening, signaling their return. I'd run around furiously trying to make up for the time I'd squandered. My procrastination would suddenly be cured. The consequences of disobedience had not changed, but the proximity of the punishment had! My parents' imminent return served as powerful motivation. This is the same kind of appeal James uses to deter us from grumbling and complaining about those around us instead of exercising forbearance. If this behavior will result in judgment and the executor of the judgment is knocking at the door, then why in the world would we risk engaging in the behavior in the first place?

How much should we be willing endure without complaining? James offers the Old Testament prophets as real-life examples. He doesn't draw our attention just to their lives, but specifically to their perseverance and endurance. In the last part of the verse he recharacterizes the prophets as those "[speaking] in the name of the Lord." In doing so, James strongly suggests the provocative behavior the prophets endured was not petty foibles or bothersome habits, but something far more significant. The prophets were known for persistently proclaiming God's message in the face of (sometimes heated) opposition from those who didn't want to hear what they had to say. This does not excuse our grumbling for more petty reasons, but the reference to the prophets suggests James had more significant issues in mind.

In the first part of verse 11, James simultaneously offers a concluding summary of what precedes and sets the scene for his next example. He broadens his reference to "the prophets" to include "those who have endured"—the ones we consider blessed. Among this larger group, James naturally points to Job as his next example, again citing his patience, not just his life in general. What's the takeaway for James? How things turned out in the end. Job's story begins with all of the people and possessions in Job's life being stripped away in a rapid series of tragic events (Job 1:13–19). Job is described in 1:1 as "blameless and upright and God-fearing and turning away from evil." But Satan raises the possibility with God that Job's behavior might simply be the result of God's blessing, not of any sense of deep reverence and love for him. Based on Job's experience, the remainder of the book addresses questions about the nature of faith and relationship with God. In the end God restores Job's fortunes and richly blesses him, but it is only after he has endured untold suffering, including the "encouraging" advice of his friends (see Job 42:10).

For Example...

James 5:7,10

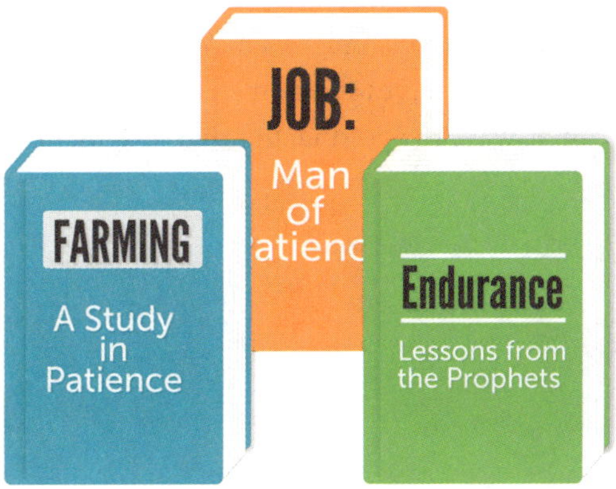

The Lord showed himself to be compassionate and merciful. Although Job may have done nothing to deserve the hardships he experienced, in the end, God met his demands with a rebuke. Nevertheless, God responded graciously to Job, restoring his fortunes. And Job's "friends"? They also experienced mercy and compassion, both from the Lord and from Job, based on his willingness to pray for them.

For Example...: In the face of hardships we cannot avert, James commands us to be patient. He offers three examples illustrating the types of outcomes we can expect when we endure. The first example, farming, draws upon our knowledge of agriculture and the expected outcome of cultivating plants. The other two come from the Old Testament. All three encourage us to resist impatiently reacting to circumstances or situations that we cannot control.

James introduces his final admonition of the section by saying "above all," which frames his warning as a capstone for the preceding arguments. The exhortation not to swear by heaven or earth or using any other kind of oath echoes what Jesus commanded his disciples in Matthew 5:34–35. Why would anyone need to swear an oath? If "yes" didn't always mean yes. Think about it: If I made promises or commitments and didn't keep them, how would people know whether I really meant what I said? Adding an oath would be like me telling my kids, "Okay, I REALLY mean it this time!" when I already told them to stop but didn't take action when they disobeyed. The need for oaths signifies a deeper problem: a failure to follow through on commitments. James gets right to the heart of the matter. Instead of bolstering your statements to make up for lack of follow-through, keep your word! Let your "yes" or "no" really mean something! It might take a while for people to accept that you have changed, but change we should. Once again, James' motivational appeal for change is impending judgment.

The theme of impending judgment flows throughout this section. It serves as encouragement for those who are suffering to be patient. But it also serves as an ominous warning to those who need to change their ways to avoid facing that judgment.

James 5:13–20

It is common at the end of New Testament letters for the writers to speed up the pace of their instruction. More pressing matters requiring more detailed explanation tend to be handled earlier, whereas their final commands are usually fairly self-explanatory, with little detail. Such is the case with James. All the letters focus on the positive use of the tongue (praying, singing praise, advising), unlike the negative examples offered throughout James' letter (e.g., 1:19, 26; 3:1–12; 4:11; 5:12).

James presents a series of issues and solutions, with the third one featuring a descriptive sidebar about sickness and healing. The extended description in verses 16c–18 can make it seem as though verse 19 begins a new section in its own right, one dealing with the fourth issue. This notion is tempting based on the apparent disconnect between dealing with someone who has wandered from the truth and the example of Elijah's powerful prayer. But the introduction of the final issue in verse 19 follows the same pattern as those in verses 13–16, so this section is best understood as one unit. Now let's take a look at each part in turn.

James introduces each situation by asking rhetorical questions. Is anyone suffering misfortune? Is anyone cheerful? Is anyone sick? James is not polling his audience, expecting them to raise their hands in response. What he means would be much more like asking, "How should we respond when we're suffering misfortune? We should pray. And when we're cheerful? We should sing praise."

By asking these questions, James creates an opportunity to offer commands. He could have just as easily given the commands first followed by the situation: "Pray when you are suffering misfortune!" What's the difference? The questions he asks here give us a chance to think about possible answers before James offers his. As we see from his use of them elsewhere, rhetorical questions are an elegant way of introducing situations in order to offer solutions—just as we see with prayer being offered as the response for misfortune, sickness, and forgiveness.

The first situation James mentions in verse 13 is suffering misfortune of some kind, though he offers no specifics. James uses the verbal form of the same word he used in verse 10 to describe the example of the prophets, translated generally as "suffering" or "perseverance." It applies to being in the midst of unpleasant circumstances, ones that we would rather avoid. In verse 10, James holds up the prophets as a model of endurance for us to follow. Here in verse 13, he commands a response that helps ensure we will indeed endure: prayer.

James relies on his previous teaching about how we ought to ask for things in prayer; he offers no new advice. Recall that in 1:5–7, he challenges the person asking for wisdom to believe and not doubt, lest they miss out on what they ask for. In 4:2–3, he addresses motivation for asking in prayer. If we ask with the wrong motives—like fulfilling our selfish desires—we should not expect to receive anything. His previous teaching about prayer thus serves as a backdrop for the exhortation to pray as we encounter suffering. So, too, does the knowledge that the testing of our faith through trials builds endurance and leads to maturity (1:3–4).

James then turns to times of being cheerful and in good spirits. What's the fitting response? Singing praise! This is the first mention of cheerfulness or praise in the book, although there are others references to joy (1:2; 4:9). Based on James' command to consider trials pure joy, the first reference reminds us that rejoicing is a choice, not an emotion. Later in chapter 4, James warns the rich that their laughter and joy should be turned to mourning in light of the coming judgment they face.

His omission of "among you" in the second part of verse 13 links it more closely to the first part, creating a contrasting portrait of responses to situations we encounter. James seems to say here that we should expect to encounter both suffering and cheer, or perhaps that some members of the congregation may be experiencing one while others experience the opposite.

In verse 14, James offers a more thorough description and solution—a procedure, to be followed in the case of sickness, that we moderns have largely forsaken except in extreme cases. Our first inclination today is to consult a doctor without considering the spiritual implications of sickness. This is not to say that James excludes the notion of medical help. Rather, he is highlighting the significant spiritual problem that sickness poses. He offers a practical example of how a community of believers can respond to a brother or sister in special need. Will they respond by exhibiting both faith and works, or will they offer just a "hope you get better, we'll be praying" response akin to what James presented in 2:15–17? The sick are vulnerable just like those who are poor, widowed, and orphaned (1:27).

So what does faith in action look like in the context of sickness? The process James describes begins with a call to the elders for help. They, in turn, respond with prayer for the sick one and anoint them with oil, much like the disciples are described as doing in Mark 6:13. Sickness provides opportunity for individuals and communities to exercise their faith through their ministry to one another. The call for the elders acknowledges dependence upon the larger community, and their response demonstrates the value of putting the needs of others before their own.

The second half of verse 15 shifts to forgiveness of sin, which conjures up notions about the correlation of sin and sickness like those expressed by Jesus' disciples in John 9:2.There are most definitely natural physical consequences resulting from some sins, but this does not mean that all sickness can be traced back to someone's sin. Luke Timothy Johnson makes important connection between Jesus' ministry and the forgiveness of sin: "The prayer that can raise the sick person and heal the community can also prove triumphant over the powers of evil in the world, for prayer is the openness of the human spirit to the powerful word of God that enables it to work."[1]

Prayer of Faith

James 5:14–16

Prayer of Faith: James does not recognize the distinctions we might make today between spiritual illness and physical illness. Both conditions threatened the individual and the community of believers, and both called for intervening prayer. Requesting help reflects an individual's recognition that they cannot overcome their situation alone. The response of the elders to pray for and anoint them reflects putting faith into practical action.

James draws out a principle in verse 16 from the preceding discussion: confessing our sins to one another. We might ask what this has to do with anointing a sick person as we pray for their healing, but it makes perfect sense when we think about Jesus' healing ministry. Johnson notes that both the sick and the sinner face a crisis that potentially excludes them from the community of faith. This explains the tight correlation between healing and confession/forgiveness of sin. The passive verb in verse 15b simply states that their sin will be forgiven; it does not say who will forgive that sin, so there is no reason to think it is anyone other than God. Confession of sin to others in the community of faith represents the same call for help as a sick person summoning the elders. In both situations, the individual requires care and support to restore health and to ensure that the problem does not spread to the rest of the community. This explains

1. Johnson, Luke Timothy. *The Letter of James: A New Translation with Introduction and Commentary*. Vol. 37A. Anchor Yale Bible (New Haven; London: Yale University Press, 2008), 344.

why James does not make a distinction between medical and spiritual healing like we might today.

Offering up prayers in faith is critically important, whether it be physical or spiritual healing that one seeks. This is why, in the last part of verse 16, James applies his discussion of healing both to the sick and those suffering in sin. Confession brings our struggles out into the open, where others can help us. Temptation loses much of its power as we tell others what we face. But confession also requires follow-through from the community. Failure to hold a brother or sister accountable is akin to telling them to be warmed and filled: It fails to meet the needs expressed by the confession.

What about the outcome of the prayer of faith? Does James *guarantee* healing? Some have claimed that he does, leading to added pain and shattered faith for many. The phrasing of the statements in verses 14–16 highlights the natural correlation between the action and the outcome. It's not to say that you will only be healed if you pray, nor that you'll be guaranteed healing if you do pray. He redirects our attention from ourselves and the situation to the One who is really in control.

James bolsters his claim about the impact the effective prayer of a righteous person can have by offering an example from the Old Testament. In contrast to holding up the prophets as an example of endurance in verse 10, James portrays Elijah in verse 17 as a person just like us. Although God did miraculous things through Elijah, the takeaway here is that God can do the same things through us as we pray in faith. Just as God answered Elijah's prayer for the rain to cease and then for it to begin again, he will answer us too if we ask in faith (1:6–7; 5:15–16) and with the right motives (4:2–3).

We finally come to the closing verses of the section and of the book. James' expression "my brothers" normally marks a transition to a new unit. Here, it creates a transition from the extended discussion of prayer and healing (5:14–18) to a new situation parallel to the ones introduced in verses 13a, 13b, and 14. Instead of asking a rhetorical question, James uses a conditional clause: "If anyone among you should wander...." Verse 19 and the first part of verse 20 form one long, complex sentence in Greek that introduces both the situation and the response, just as in the preceding instances. This situation has two aspects: someone wandering from the truth, and someone else turning them back to it. How should we respond? This situation calls for more of a "knowing" than a "doing" response since the intervention has already taken place in the wandering person's life.

In verse 20, we learn more about what James means by turning back someone wandering from the truth. Instead of just saying, "They will save that person's soul," James uses a new expression to characterize the person intervening. They are "the one who turns a sinner back from the error of his way." What an image! It's like stopping a blind person before they walk off a precipice!

By saying "among you," James implies here that he is referring to believers who wander away from the truth rather than those who have never accepted it. Some have taken this statement to refer more generally to unbelievers living around the believers. Like many other verses in this book, these are challenging verses to understand. If the more general audience of unbelievers is what James means, then his reference to saving their souls would be more literal, referring to salvation. If he uses "among you" to refer more narrowly to the community of believers, then his reference to saving their souls is best understood as highlighting the gravity of turning away from the truth as a believer. James is not referring to a loss of salvation, but his phrasing here is yet another example of him rattling his readers.

The one who intervenes not only saves the wanderer, but also covers over a multitude of sins. James ascribes to the intervention the same outcome as love in 1 Peter 4:8. Whose sin? At the very least, it would be the wayward sinner's. For us to turn back to the truth requires that we give up the sin that turned us away in the first place. This would account for part of the overall reduction of sin.

Another aspect of limiting sin stems from the effect one person can have on a larger community. Both 1 Corinthians 5:4–7 and Galatians 6:1 describe situations where the sin of one person has the potential to influence others to follow the same path. Paul summarizes this principle in Galatians 5:9, his famous analogy that "a little leaven leavens the whole batch of dough." Sin left unaddressed will affect the entire community. I am not talking here about a mystical spread of some kind, but a literal spread. When one person's unacceptable behavior becomes acceptable, others inevitably join in. This is why it is so critical for us, as a body of believers, to be meaningfully engaged in one another's lives. How can we call for the help of elders we have never met? Are they willing and trained to come? How can we turn back a sinner from their error if we, too, are dabbling in our own sin? Assuming we are walking in the truth, will the wanderer listen to us if we have no other relationship with them? These are difficult questions that confront the modern church—all the more as we become fragmented in our relationships.

Final Reflections

James covers a wide range of topics in his letter, but the theme of "faith in action" stands out as one thread tying it all together. Chapter 1 introduces the principle that the testing of faith is what grows and matures it, not just the mere possession of it (1:2–4). Faith is also the basis for asking for wisdom; without it we are like waves blown about (1:5–8). Next James turns the world's view of rich and poor on its head from the perspective of faith (1:9–11) before revealing the true sources of testing and good gifts (1:12–18). Regardless of how we might feel about these matters, James challenges us to accept his view.

In verses 19–27, James contrasts hearing and taking action with hearing alone. Faith requires both. He closes the section with the practical example of the damage we do with our tongues. His call to bridle our tongues makes clear that James has specific acts of faith in mind for us to do. Reckless words break faith within the community, making one's religion worthless compared with caring for widows and orphans and preserving one's purity from the world (1:26–27). Another faith-breaker within the community is showing partiality (2:1–13), basing treatment of others on the world's values of rich and poor instead of God's view as outlined in 1:9–11.

James broadens the scope of faith in action from partiality and the tongue to contrast faith and works in 2:14–26. Just as untested faith remains immature and incomplete (1:2–4), so too does faith without works (2:22). James creates a poignant portrait of just how worthless idle faith is: telling a brother or sister in need to keep themselves warm and fed while taking no practical steps to offer help (2:15–16).

What's the point of claiming faith if we never put it to work? Just as faithless religion is worthless (1:26), so too is dead faith (2:26).

In 3:1–12, James resumes his discussion of the impact that faith in action (or its absence) can have on the tongue. Although the tongue has beneficial uses like teaching and blessing, it is capable of the same devastating destruction as a wildfire (3:5–6)—yet some see no problem with blessing God at one moment and cursing fellow image-bearers the next (3:9–10). Our only hope to prevent our tongues being a source of stumbling (3:2) or oxymoronic hypocrisy (3:10–12) is to put faith in action to tame what human nature cannot (3:7). The self-control that keeps our tongue in check will have the same effect on the rest of us, leading to maturity (3:2). Putting faith in action also differentiates the truly wise from those who delude themselves (3:13–18). What's the difference? The genuinely wise exhibit humility in their good works. True and false wisdom also lead to very different kinds of fruit (3:15–18).

The inner battle of our desires is yet another opportunity where faith in action is a game-changer (4:1–10). Instead of blaming our struggles on external sources, James challenges us to address the role that envy and selfish desires play in our conflicts. Instead of worshiping idols created by our own desires, we should direct our spirits to the God, who jealously desires us to worship him. Thankfully, God's grace is there for us as we humbly turn to him (4:5–6). Drawing near to God leads to a reciprocal response from him; humbling ourselves leads to God exalting us; resisting the devil leads to him fleeing from us (4:7–10). James closes the chapter by challenging us to consider whether we look to God for what he would have us do, or presumptuously make our own plans without divine consideration (4:13–16). Pursuing our own plans in lieu of the good God would have us do is sin, period (4:17).

James begins the final chapter with a challenge to consider how faith in action affects our investment strategy. Although directed at the rich, the principles he outlines undermine any confidence anyone might place in the lasting value of riches. Instead of a profitable investment, they turn out to be toxic assets that bear witness against us. How? By diverting them from where God intended—like helping those in need (2:15–16)—or by withholding wages that are due to fund self-indulgent lifestyles (5:3–5). For those currently suffering from the economic fallout of such behavior, James exhorts us to be patient (5:7). We can be confident as we wait because of the nearness of the Lord's return, when all such matters will be judged and rectified (5:8). His imminent return should also deter us from complaining against one another or equivocating on the truth to the point that we must swear an oath to be taken seriously (5:9, 12).

The closing picture of faith in action focuses on life within a community of faith. Those suffering from sickness should ask for help, and the community around them must respond in faith (5:13–14). Why? The prayer of faith can accomplish both physical and spiritual healing (5:15). This is our motivation to confess our sins to and to pray for one another (5:16). James challenges us to recognize that the health of the individual, be it physical or spiritual, affects the health of the entire community. James closes with an illustration of members turning wandering believers back to the truth (5:19–20).

James teaches us that acquiring faith and wisdom is admirable, but it is only the beginning. Unless we humbly apply them and withstand the tests that come our way, we will never bear the fruit that God intended. Faith that is never put into action is dead, and the religion that it fosters is worthless. Self-serving is not divine, but demonic.

James' challenge to us is not simply, "Got faith?" He wants to know what we are doing with it—and so does God, whose return is ever nearer. How are we going to respond to this challenge? By humbling ourselves before God and walking in the grace he offers us.

About the Author

Steven E. Runge serves as a scholar-in-residence at Faithlife. He has a Doctor of Literature degree in biblical languages from the University of Stellenbosch in South Africa, supervised by Christo Van der Merwe. He currently serves as a research associate affiliated with the Department of Ancient Studies, University of Stellenbosch. In preparation for his doctoral research, Steve completed several years of study in the linguistic fields of pragmatics and discourse grammar. This culminated in attending a workshop on discourse analysis offered by SIL/Wycliffe Bible Translators, facilitated by Stephen H. Levinsohn. He has also earned a Master of Theological Studies degree in biblical languages from Trinity Western Seminary in Langley, B.C., and a BA in speech communication from Western Washington University.

Steve has served as a visiting professor teaching Greek discourse grammar at Knox Theological Seminary; Dallas Theological Seminary, Wycliffe Hall, Oxford; Wales Evangelical School of Theology; and Southern Baptist Theological Seminary, besides offering exegesis workshops for pastors. While completing his education, Steve served as an adjunct faculty member at Northwest Baptist Theological College, Trinity Western University, and Associated Canadian Theological Schools (ACTS). He and his wife were married in 1990. They have two daughters and live in Bellingham.

Subject and Author Index

G

H

I

J

K

L

M

P

Scripture Index

Ephesians

Philippians

Colossians

1 Timothy

Hebrews

James

1 Peter

Revelation